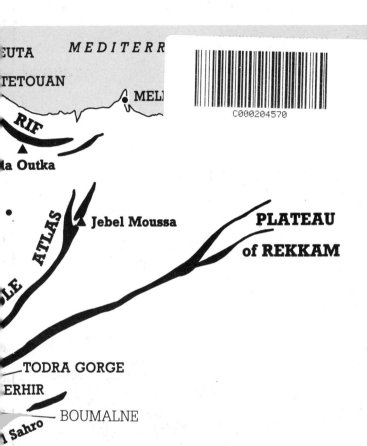

EUTA

*MEDITERR*

TETOUAN

MEL

RIF

▲
la Outka

▲ Jebel Moussa

**PLATEAU**

OLE ATLAS

of REKKAM

TODRA GORGE

ERHIR

BOUMALNE

l Sahro

# MOROCCO
# PRINCIPAL RANGES

E

600 km

# THE ATLAS MOUNTAINS

*Fortified storehouse, Tessaout Valley*

# THE ATLAS MOUNTAINS

## A WALKER'S GUIDE

### KARL SMITH

CICERONE PRESS
MILNTHORPE, CUMBRIA, U.K.

## Acknowledgements

Space permits me to mention only a few of the many people who have helped me write this book. For those who accompanied me on numerous trips and made my time in Morocco so enjoyable, thanks also.

I would especially like to thank: Jan Campbell, Alice England, Alan Keohane, Pam Lucas, Maureen McMurtry, Steve Parker, Mike Wynn, and Peter the truck driver (whose surname escapes me).

Karl Smith

## Advice to Readers

Readers are advised that whilst every effort is taken by the author to ensure the accuracy of this guidebook, changes can occur which may affect the contents. It is advisable to check locally on transport, accommodation, shops etc but even rights-of-way can be altered.

The publisher would welcome notes of any such changes

# Contents

*Tissili village*

# PART ONE
## Introduction

### The Appeal of the Atlas

Pliny, the great Roman geographer, on seeing the Atlas peaks described them as "the most fabulous mountains in all of Africa." Stretching southwards from the Mediterranean coast in an arc for a thousand miles, they are certainly the highest and most extensive range in North Africa.

For the walker and mountaineer they offer an incredible variety of scenery, climate and terrain. Within the valleys one can observe a way of life that has changed little during the last thousand years; the word unique can be used with justification. Whilst the wild scenery may be reminiscent of parts of Central Asia, a closer look at the way of life here dispels any such notion. The native inhabitants of this region, the Berbers, possess a distinctive culture. Their villages of kasbahs, surrounded by steep terraces, are of a special beauty, and leave a lasting impression on the visitor.

Exploration of these mountains by Europeans began in earnest with the arrival of French colonists, and their long presence here means that all but the most insignificant summits have been ascended. Nowadays, the area around Jebel Toubkal and its approaches has established itself as a popular destination for walkers from all over Europe. Journey beyond these narrow confines, however, and one is unlikely to meet anyone other than the native Berber inhabitants.

Whilst opportunities for rock-climbing do exist (and some very good opportunities they are too), this book is primarily aimed at the walker and scrambler. Whatever one's age or level of fitness the Atlas mountains are a rewarding and exciting destination, easily reached from Europe.

This book covers the Toubkal region, which contains the highest and most spectacular peaks, and also describes a circuit of the less well-known but equally impressive Mgoun massif area. Other areas of interest are described briefly.

*Lower Dades Gorges*

## The Geography and Geology of the Atlas
### Geography
The Atlas mountains form several ranges, as follows:

The High (or Grand) Atlas run roughly ENE from the Atlantic coast near Agadir as far as northern Algeria, where they diminish and curve eastwards, forming the Saharan Atlas. In the central High Atlas, another range strikes north-eastward. This is the Middle Atlas, the main watershed of the country. At the southern end of the High Atlas, a separate range runs parallel to the south and east. This is the Anti-Atlas. Jebel Sahro forms the eastern end of this range, and is separated from both the main Atlas chain and the Anti-Atlas by the Dades valley, which runs into the main Drâa valley. Further south, the High Atlas and Anti-Atlas are separated by a broad, fertile valley known as the Souss. Finally, there are the Rif mountains, parallel to the Mediterranean coast in the north.

The High Atlas hold the most interest for the walker, and form the bulk of this book. South and east of Marrakech two motor roads cross the High Atlas via passes. These are the Tizi-n'Test to the west, and the Tizi-n'Tichka to the east and they form the boundaries of the Toubkal Atlas. Immediately to the east lies the Central High Atlas, a large area which extends as far as the Plateau des Lacs and Imilchil. This region contains the M'goun massif and the fertile Ait Bougoumez valley.

Returning west, beyond the Tizi-n'Test one enters the Western High Atlas. This remote area has much to offer the walker. Whilst lacking the highest peaks, there are several interesting summits, up to 3,551m in height (Jbel Tinergwet).

## Geology

During the carboniferous era marine Palaeozoic sediments were affected by severe pressure, resulting in intense folding and mountain building (this Hercynean orogeny was also responsible for much European mountain formation), which was then eroded to a flat or gently undulating peneplain. The second phase in the Atlas development resulted in further wearing down and the deposition of sediments. The third phase, beginning in the middle of the tertiary period, started with renewed folding, resulting in the mountains as we know them today. The folding was accompanied by down-sinking, leading to the formation of basins such as the Souss, and by volcanic eruptions. Jebel Siroua is an example of the latter. The fourth phase added little to what previously existed. Torrential erosion has thrown thick alluvial deposits over the basins at the foot of the Atlas.

In the Toubkal area the rock consists of volcanic green andesites, rhyolites and tuffs. These are ancient rocks laid bare, forming the characteristic jagged peaks and steep-sided valleys. Detritus suggests that small glaciers may have existed in the higher cirques, but otherwise the area was not glaciated (as can be deduced from the numerous spurs which project into the valleys). In places what appears to be moraine, is usually debris from landslips. The village of Aroumd is built on such debris, from what must have been an enormous landslip.

The Central High Atlas are characterised by extensive outcrops of fairly soft permian-triassic strata. They are simply folded rock structures, with broad open synclines and sharp anticlines (e.g.

Jebel Ghat). In places rivers have cut down through the soft rock to produce deep gorges, another characteristic feature in the Mgoun area. The Jebel Sahro and Anti-Atlas are of a totally different origin and structure. They are part of the great elevated mass of the African plateau, and are formed of old schists and hard quartzites.

## Climate - When to Go

It is possible to walk and climb in the Atlas throughout the year. Despite the proximity to the Sahara the summer temperatures in the mountains are bearable. Whilst it can reach 130°F at midday in Marrakech, up in the hills it may only be a pleasant 70°F. Walking in the lower valleys can, however, be rather hot. At night it rarely gets chilly except on the higher peaks.

The best time to visit is probably in late spring. At this time the winter snows have not melted, and this makes the going underfoot much easier. It is warm enough during the day to be in shirt sleeves, although at night a good sleeping bag is needed. In autumn the weather becomes noticeably cooler and towards the end of September snow showers can be expected on the higher peaks. At this time of year there is abundant ripe fruit in the valleys, a welcome addition to the diet. Early winter is a time best avoided: cold, often wet and without the benefit of firm snow underfoot. Late winter can give some of the finest days here, warm with clear skies, when skiing and sunbathing are both equally possible. On bad winter days a warm duvet may be useful as it can get down to -20°C.

Storms can occur at any time of the year, but in summer they are infrequent and do give plenty of warning of their approach. Rain turns to snow on the higher peaks by October. Temperatures on these peaks can be decidedly chilly, even in mid-summer if there is any wind about. Toubkal is notorious in this respect and anyone choosing to bivvy here can expect frost throughout the year.

## Flora and Fauna
### Flora
One of the most noticeable features of the Atlas is their barrenness, yet despite this there is a wide variety of interesting plants to be seen. Most famous of the trees is, perhaps, the Atlas cedar *(Cedrus*

*The Tessaout Gorge*

*atlanticus).* The former extensive forests are now sadly gone from the High Atlas, though still to be found in the Middle Atlas and Rif. Elsewhere the thuya *(Arbor-vitae)* is often found on the lower slopes, together with juniper.

In the limestone areas of the Atlas many of the familiar herbs are to be found, such as lavender, rosemary and thyme. The dry terraces are covered in thorny scrub, the result of centuries of over-grazing. Many of the flowers are similar, or identical, to those found in the Mediterranean regions. The best time to observe these flowers is in the spring, when the winter snows have just melted. Narcissi and crocuses are followed by squill and asphodel. Kermes oak, arbutus, wormwood, lentisk, myrtle and mastic dominate the lower slopes of the Atlas.

Whilst a comprehensive description of the flora is beyond the scope of this book, those interested should refer to *Catalogue des Plants du Maroc* by Jahandiez, E. & Negre, R. or *L'Afrique du Nord* by Marie, R. (illustrated).

## Fauna

The Atlas are very sparsely populated with wildlife. Most likely to be encountered is the Barbary ground-squirrel, (there are also wild boar, gazelle and Barbary apes). Beyond that one may be fortunate and sight a mouflon, the large-horned sheep which still exists here. It is possible that leopards also still exist; lions only disappeared in 1922. Snakes and reptiles, including chameleons, are numerous. Of the insects the Atlas are home to several endemic species of butterfly, the one most likely to be encountered being the giant grayling *(Berberia abdelkader).*

Very rewarding for the naturalist is the birdlife: amongst the species endemic to the area are the Barbary partridge, and Levaillant's green woodpecker *(P. vaillantii).* In the cities and towns the common bulbul is both frequent and noisy. Other notable sights include rollers *(Coracias garrulus),* abundant in places such as the Ait Bougoumez valley, while booted and Bonelli's eagle are not uncommon. The mountains of the High Atlas are the home of the lammergeier *(Gypetus barbatus)* and Egyptian vulture. Choughs and Alpine choughs are common and on the plains heading towards the hills one can see egrets, sand-grouse, and the elusive great bustard.

The Jebel Sahro region has a noticeably more exotic avian fauna. Several species of sandgrouse occur (though more heard than seen) and the rock towers of the Taggourt plateau are a good place to see the Barbary falcon.

For further information see bibliography.

## History and Culture - the Berbers

Rock-carvings found in the Atlas indicate that this area has been inhabited for at least 12,000 years. The first inhabitants were the Berbers, who still constitute a large part of the population of Morocco, and are by far the dominant ethnic group in the mountain regions.

The origins of the Berbers are unclear. They are believed by some to be Caucasian in origin, to have crossed the straights of Gibraltar from Europe and spread gradually throughout North-West Africa (the Maghreb). Elements in their architecture, still unchanged in the mountains today, link them to Pharaonic Egypt. On the other

*Sidi Chamarouch*

*Waterseller
Djemaa el Fna*

hand lozenges and chevrons found today on rugs reflect early Asian, or southern European designs, as does the pottery.

Very early in their history the Berbers were divided into three major tribes; the Sanhajas, Zenatas and the Masmoudas. Of these the Masmoudas were the ones who settled in the Atlas, Rif and Anti-Atlas as farmers, while the other tribes adopted a nomadic existence.

During the Roman occupation of North Africa, known by them as Mauretania, the Berbers were left largely untouched. Originally

14

practising agrarian, animistic religions (some of which may have been adopted by the Romans) they were subsequently 'converted' to Judaism. This was at best a nominal conversion, possibly manufactured by Jews who (as part of the great dispersion) fled to Morocco after the destruction of the temple in AD 70. The Jews remained in Morocco through the centuries, forming a small but influential community with its own specific identity.

With the arrival of St. Cyprian, the Berbers 'converted' to Christianity, although once again this was very loosely practised. It was not until the arrival of Islam that the Berbers found a religion to which they adhered strictly. Today, the Berbers are almost universally muslim, of the Shi'ite sect.

Islam came with the Arab invasion of the Maghreb at the end of the seventh century. This produced lasting changes in Morocco where the Arabs are today, by and large, the ruling race. Whilst the Berbers took to Islam they did not accept Arab rule so readily, nor did they adopt Arabic as their language.

During the years following the Arab invasion, the ever-increasing tide of Islam took Arab and Berber alike into Spain, where they remained until the fall of Granada in 1492. By this stage Morocco had become an isolated, backward-looking country divided into two kingdoms: Fez and Marrakech (the name Morocco is in fact a corruption of 'Marrakech'). So it was to remain for the next few centuries, succumbing to the influence of Turkey and being invaded variously by Portugal and Spain. Then, towards the latter part of the nineteenth century, a new influence made itself felt in Morocco; the arrival of the French. By 1912 the country had become a French protectorate. For the next forty years the French introduced civil reforms, constructed railways and roads, and greatly expanded the economy. This came to an end in 1956 when Morocco was formally granted independence under Mohammed V.

Today the French presence has dwindled to a fraction of its former level, although the French who remain are often in important positions. Morocco is now an independent monarchy under Hassan II. Much of this recent history has, however, failed to influence the way of life of the Berbers who have remained isolated from the economic and social progress Morocco has made.

15

*Ruined Kasbah, Dades valley*

### Berber Architecture

No guide to the Atlas would be complete without a mention of the local architecture. The first sight of a Berber hill village removes any illusion a visitor may have of still being in Europe. The cubic, flat-topped village houses of mud or stone stand out against the steep hillsides and give the Atlas their unique character. In parts of the Atlas, and in the valleys to the south, the famous kasbahs are still to be found. These buildings are of indeterminate age - one thinks of the Glaouis' fortress, now in decay, which, although relatively modern, has every appearance of dating back to the Middle Ages. The village houses with their wood drainage-gutters, wooden locks and flat earth roofs reinforce this impression. In a country where transport is difficult it is inevitable that the architecture reflects the materials closest to hand in its construction. In the Atlas one therefore finds buildings made of mud, stone, and above all *pisé*, the local mud pressed between wooden boards and dried. Most of the kasbahs are constructed of this material.

Whilst in the Toubkal region one encounters little other than flat-topped, straight-sided village houses, in areas such as the Mgoun and Anti-Atlas one finds the more characteristic examples of Maghreb architecture. The buildings of interest can be divided into three sorts; the kasbah, the ksar and the agadir. The kasbah, the most frequently encountered, is a tall fortified house of square ground-plan, with distinctive tapering walls. These are pierced by narrow slits similar to lancet windows in a medieval castle. The four corners are usually projecting. The ksar (plural ksour) is more commonly found to the SE of the High Atlas (e.g. Risani, Erfoud), and is more definitely a sort of Roman castrum, being oblong and surrounded by an unbroken wall of even height. Finally, the agadirs are great grain storehouses, of major importance to the villagers. These can be seen, for example, in the Tessaout valley.

The origins of the architecture of the kasbah, which is unique in form, lie in the tribal existence which prevailed here for millenia as the tribes grew from extended families to units of several families. Clearly defensive in function, the whole family together with its livestock could shelter inside its kasbah in times of intercommunal strife. The watchtowers at each corner of the kasbah served to warn of enemy approach.

Stylistically the origins of this architecture are harder to determine. There are two main areas where it is believed to have come from. Firstly Yemen, the former Arabia Felix, where the present-day buildings are somewhat similar in proportion, and secondly Pharoanic Egypt, where the pyramids, temples and other sloping-walled buildings may, some experts believe, have served as inspiration. It was the Arabs, however, who brought to Morocco the peculiar tapering kasbah tower-shape. The first examples of such structures in the Maghreb are in the minarets of the mosques at Kairouan (670 AD) and at Sfax (9th cent.). The enclosing walls and patio forming the centre of the kasbah main house are thought to have their origins in the Roman-Byzantine castellum. The actual Roman castrum is believed to have influenced the ksour rather than the kasbah. It is the Islamic influence, from the Persian (Sassanid) and Abbasid dynasties, that affects the ornamentation, in particular, the rectangular brick patterns of projecting and receding bricks.

*Typical tiled decoration*

These were reproduced in mud or *pisé* by the Berbers, who lacked the skills needed for brickwork (although a fine example in brick can, in fact, be seen on the Koutoubia minaret in Marrakech).

However, despite all these influences the kasbahs do deserve to be called solely Berber. They have no Persian domes, arches from Rome or circular ornamentation; created to suit particular local requirements they are far more original than imitative.

## Using this Book

The walking times given for routes described in this book allow for brief rests, but do not include lunch stops. However, the times specified are, in the main, fairly generous. Much of the walking I have done in Morocco has been with large groups, some of whom have not been particularly fit, and times are based on such groups. A fit party or individual would have no trouble fitting more into their schedule than that outlined in the book.

The direction L(eft) and R(ight) refer to the walker's direction of travel, unless stated otherwise.

As regards place names I have used those that appear on the 1:50,000 and 1:100,000 maps. Where these differ between maps I have used the more popular (usually older) name.

All routes and times are described as done in summer. In winter and spring, snow cover will make any of the scree routes much quicker and easier (e.g. Ascent of Toubkal).

Finally, prices change, especially in a country of high inflation such as Morocco. All prices given are those found in 1997, at an exchange rate of 15.07 Dirhams (Drh.) = £1, with 1 Dirham, effectively, exactly equivalent to 7 pence.

*Village girl*

*Aroumd*

# PART TWO
## Practical Information

## Getting There

By Air: there are flights to Marrakech via Casablanca daily from London, cost approx. £311+£26 tax (1997). Operators - Royal Air Maroc (reservations tel. 0171 439 4361. Air France also flies this route, via Paris. With Royal Air Maroc it is necessary to reconfirm flights at least 72 hours before departure, best done on arrival in Marrakech (Offices in Hotel Asni).

A cheaper alternative is to find a charter flight to Agadir. There are international airports in Tangier, Fez and Rabat as well as Marrakech. Probably the cheapest way of all, if time allows, is to find a cheap charter flight to Málaga, take a bus to Algeciras where a ferry runs to Tangier. This can also be done with flights to Gibraltar.

Overland: with the advent of cheap charter flights, overland travel has been largely superseded. In the early days, when Ramblers ran treks in the Atlas, travel was by train! It is still a long journey today, taking around 3 days to reach Marrakech from London. It may, however, be worthwhile for someone travelling with an Inter-rail pass. Long-distance buses operate a regular service to Málaga, from where the local bus and ferry can be taken as described above.

Ferry crossings to Morocco run from Algeciras to Tangier, Ceuta and Mellila (the latter two being Spanish enclaves). From Gibraltar to Tangier a hydrofoil runs as well as a ferry.

Finally, there is a ferry from Sète in Southern France to Tangier (38 hours, every 4 days).

With all the above modes of transport prices change and you are advised to shop around for the best bargain.

## Travel within the Country

By rail: Morocco has a relatively modern rail-network which, whilst not extensive, is cheap and fairly comfortable. Trains run from

Tangier via Rabat and Casablanca to Marrakech.

By bus: there is an excellent bus-network throughout Morocco at both local and long-distance level. They are invariably crowded; however, long-distance buses between the major cities are usually air-conditioned and comfortable. Buses are usually the cheapest method of transport (other than hitching).

By taxi: there are two types of taxi within cities; *petit taxis* and *grand taxis*. The petit taxis take 3 passengers maximum, most are fitted with meters, none of them works. Either negotiate the fare beforehand, or if you know the going rate just hand this to the driver. The latter approach often results in arguments but the driver has no real grounds for complaint.

The same rules apply for the grand taxis, which hold 5 people. Rates are twice those of the petit taxis. Unlike the petit taxis, however, they can operate on long-distance trips. It is essential to negotiate rates for such a trip beforehand. In addition there are the service taxis. These operate on fixed routes and depart when the taxi is full; often they are just large taxis, but sometimes pick-up trucks. They are much cheaper than taxis and operate in areas where there is no conventional bus service.

By car: driving in Morocco is not without its headaches. The principal routes owe their existence to the French, and are well surfaced although even here an oncoming truck or bus forces one onto the hard-shoulder. This consists of dirt and gravel, and the edge is often very pot-holed.

Other hazards include fallen rocks (very common) and wandering animals. The Moroccans have a habit of surrounding a broken-down vehicle with large stones and then leaving the stones when the vehicle is towed away.

After reading the above, you may not feel much like hiring a car, but usually a trip to Morocco passes without incident. The advantages of a hire-car, if you can afford one (it is expensive), are that it enables you to travel quickly into remote areas. Petrol is cheaper in Morocco than in Britain.

Finally, a mention must be made of hitching. This is usually very easy, although common-sense dictates that care should be exercised: keep hold of your baggage, and under no circumstances try hitching if single and female. You may well be expected to make a contribution to the driver on dismounting, in any event this should not be more than the equivalent local bus fare. Hitch-hiking is a recognised mode of transport in Morocco and is used frequently by locals.

## Visa Requirements

No visas are required for holders of a full UK visitor's passport. For other nationalities check with your embassy or travel agent.

If taking a car you need a national driving licence, together with an international driving permit for Spain and a 'green card' insurance certificate.

## Marrakech

Marrakech is one of the four imperial cities and a former capital of the country (its name is the same as 'Morocco'). At least a thousand years old it first became a town of importance during the Almoravid dynasty in the eleventh century. It was during this period that the first Koutoubia mosque was built. The minaret (of later date) still dominates the skyline of Marrakech and makes a useful central reference point.

Marrakech is invariably the starting point for trips to the Toubkal region, clearly visible from the city during the winter months. It also makes the most sensible starting point for visits to the Mgoun area and Jebel Sahro.

The city can roughly be divided into 2 parts: the old part, within the medieval ramparts, is known as the Medina; the modern French quarter is called Guêliz. Within the Medina there is an enormous souk, - a labyrinth of small shops and narrow alleyways where it is very easy to get lost. The souk is bordered on its south side by a square, the Djemaa el Fna (literally 'meeting place of the dead.') This is the main focal-point for entertainment in Marrakech. In the evenings this square comes alive with acrobats, fortune tellers, fire-eaters and dancers. Whilst some of the acts are certainly there for the western tourists, the bulk of them are intended for Moroccans (this is particularly true of the storytellers). A visit here is an absolute 'must' whilst in Marrakech, sit and observe it all from the

# MARRAKECH

1  Djemma el Fna
2  Koutoubia mosque
3  Bab er Robb
4  Ave. des Nations Unies
5  Bab Agnoaou
6  Royal Palace
7  Saadian Tombs
8  National Tourist Office

SOUK

SIDI BEL ABBES

KALA

M E D I N A

Hotel Mamounia

MELLAH

OUARZAZATE

KASBAH

Dar
Beida

Agdal Gardens

FEZ

AGADIR

N

25

*Fortune-tellers, Djemaa el Fna*

relative peace of one of the café terraces which border the square.

## Getting Around
From the airport a petit taxi to the city centre is 40-80 Drh.
Negotiate the price beforehand. The main local bus station is
located on the street leading off the Djemaa el Fna towards the Hotel
Foucauld. Petit taxis are cheap; don't worry if they are already
occupied, the driver will usually stop for you. Mention should also
be made of the horse-drawn carriages or *calèches* which are a
feature of Marrakech. By no means there solely for the tourist trade,
they are used by Marrakchis as taxis. They are slower than, but a
similar price to, petit taxis.

## Accommodation
This ranges from the lowest flea-pit in the Medina to world-class
hotels like the Mamounia. There is a decent, patrolled campsite
near the new quarter on the edge of the city. It is best to take a taxi
there. For cheap hotels look in the streets near the Djemaa el Fna,

across from the Souk. The Hotel C.M.T., directly by the bus station, is cheap and popular. Slightly upmarket from this and very popular with trekking groups is the Hotel Foucauld. It is situated 300 yards from the Djemaa el Fna on Ave. el Mouahidine, to the left of the Koutoubia. There is also a youth hostel in Marrakech.

## Supplies

For all treks, it is advisable to buy provisions in Marrakech, where there is a greater variety and reasonable prices. Unless you wish to haggle and end up paying more don't buy food in the Medina, go to the European market in Guêliz (Avenue Mohammed V, taxi 10-15 Drh., no.1 bus 80 centimes).

**N.B.** It is not possible to change money in the mountains, ensure that you change sufficient in Marrakech!

## Leaving Marrakech

The main bus station is the Bab Doukkala, situated on the NW edge of the old city walls, reached by heading NE from the Place de la Liberté. Go here for buses to Ait Mohamed, the Souss and Dades valley, and for any of the other Moroccan cities. However buses to Asni and the Toubkal region depart from the Bab er Robb bus station situated just behind the Hotel Foucauld. Buses from here to Asni at least 8 times daily, price 20 Drh.

The train station is situated on the outskirts of town to the NW.

## Sleeping and Eating
### Accommodation

Warm summer nights in the Atlas mean no worries over accommodation, one can just sleep under the stars. Either side of high summer a bivvy bag may be useful in the unlikely event of rain at night. What rain there is usually falls during the afternoon thunderstorms.

The populous nature of the Atlas means that one is usually never very far from a village or Azib (summer hut). Accommodation can nearly always be found in a village house, for a small charge. This often presents a delightful insight into the Berber way of life, and every visitor to the region should spend at least one night in a village

*Marrakech - first rain for 4 months*

house. They are normally fairly clean, if primitive. The only problem is the occasional flea or louse.

Within the Toubkal region, the Club Alpin Français (CAF) maintains a series of mountain huts (see area notes for location). All the huts provide mattress accommodation and cooking facilities, though none supply food (with the exception of Oukaimeden in winter, when it is used as a ski centre and rates are much higher). Fanta and Coca-Cola can nearly always be purchased at these huts. 1997 rates: c. 60 Drh. per night. Discounts are available to CAF, BMC and Austrian Alpine Club members on production of membership card).

There is little point carrying a tent in summer. Except in winter, accommodation can be found in villages throughout the Toubkal area. On the Mgoun massif circuit described only the two nights below Mgoun itself are spent in the open, whether a tent is carried is a matter of choice (it can be very cold and wet there in spring and autumn). In Jebel Sahro winter and early spring visits need a tent, at other times of the year bivvy bags will suffice.

*Walking up the Tessaout Valley near Ichbakene*

During winter in the Toubkal region the Lepiney refuge (q.v.) is closed. The Azibs used on the circuit described are also abandoned and frequently buried under snow. A tent is therefore necessary if one ventures away from the villages and Neltner hut (q.v.).

## Food on Trek

The staple diet of the Berbers consists of *tajine,* a stew of vegetables and mutton cooked in a conical eathenware pot. *Cous-cous,* a mix of vegetables and meat served with semolina, is also commonly eaten. If travelling singly or in a pair it is often possible to eat in village houses. Bear in mind, though, that it is largely a subsistence economy and there is thus little surplus. Passing through villages it is usually possible to buy bread, eggs and the occasional onion or potato. Beyond this it is wisest to come supplied with provisions bought in Marrakech. What little fresh food there is is often exorbitantly priced - I have been charged £5 for a small marrow! In autumn the situation is better, fresh apples and walnuts are available in the lower villages at reasonable prices.

A few villages have little stores which have a remarkably uniform line in stock. As Morocco is one of the world's largest sardine exporters it is not surprising to find shelves full of these. Biscuits, Moroccan tea, soft drinks and tins of olives form the bulk of the remaining stock. Several of the shops also sell cooking oil, nuts, powdered milk, *vache qui rit* processed cheese and tinned fruit.

It is worth mentioning another dish one may encounter if invited into a Berber home. Apart from copious quantities of mint tea, a *mechwi* may be served on special occasions, this consists of large pieces of barbecued lamb, with a whole sheep being consumed on special occasions.

## Cooking

There is no fuel for fires, it has to be collected from distant hillsides by the local inhabitants. In the villages the sort of fuel one encounters is Butagaz. Unfortunately the cylinders are too large to contemplate carrying, but if one has hired a mule, they are ideal. The bottles are cheap to purchase and refill and are freely exchangeable.

*Bread-making, village house, Amsakrou*

The initial cylinders are best purchased in Marrakech, together with a screw-in burner attachment (very cheap).

**N.B.** Ensure that you are **not** getting camping gaz. These are not exchangeable in the mountains and you could find yourself carrying useless empty cylinders around for the duration of the trip. If one carries a backpacking stove fuel will have to be bought in Marrakech.

Finally, (Toubkal region only) one could get by with using the gas in the refuges, and either eating in village houses or living on cold food for the rest of the time (no problem in summer), and mint tea is usually available.

**What to Take**

As mentioned in the introduction, do not be fooled by the proximity to the Sahara, or the temperatures in Marrakech; it often gets cold high in the mountains.

Parties visiting until the end of June should ensure they each have an ice-axe. Crampons are also essential for winter and early

30

spring, and advisable until late June.

In summer, lightweight clothes are needed for the valleys, whilst a warm sweater and waterproof jacket should be carried for the peaks. Autumn and spring need the addition of woolly hat and gloves, plus another jersey. Winter necessitates full cold-weather gear, with mountain boots, gaiters and preferably a duvet jacket.

As regards footwear, except when crampons need to be worn, a pair of lightweight hiking boots suffices. Ones with canvas uppers are ideal - there is no need for watertight boots. Gaiters, or even better, stop-touts, are useful on the long scree descents.

The ultra-violet is very intense here, and an adequate supply of high-factor sunscreen and glacier cream should be carried. Likewise, good sunglasses or snow goggles should be worn. A sunhat is essential during the summer months.

As regards sleeping bags - a lightweight bag is adequate during summer. Winter bivvies clearly necessitate a four season bag.

Tents are a matter of choice - in summer it is nice to sleep under the stars, though at other times of the year rain can be expected occasionally. A good compromise is a Gore-tex or similar bivvy bag.

An adequate supply of water purifying tablets is essential, these are unobtainable in Morocco. Disposable hand wipes, e.g. Wet Ones are also useful.

There is abundant scrambling and many alpine-style ridges; those who are competent may well wish to take a rope and basic rock gear (several krabs, slings and belt or harness). Additionally the circuit of the Mgoun massif includes an optional gorge walk which involves some climbing: rope and basic gear required for this.

For cooking, see *Sleeping and Eating.*

## Health Matters

There are no compulsory vaccinations for Morocco, though polio, tetanus, typhoid and cholera are strongly advised. Also recommended is a injection against hepatitis A.

Malaria is found in Morocco, supposedly only in the lowland areas of the far south-west of the country. Some people take prophylactic tablets, most don't. I have never heard of anyone contracting malaria in the Atlas mountains.

Bilharzia is a risk in parts of Morocco, though once again this is not known to occur in the High Atlas. It may be a risk in areas such as the Jebel Sahro, however, and the visitor is advised to exercise caution. Avoid wading or standing in still water if possible. **Under no circumstances** should water be drunk without first sterilising with tablets or by boiling.

The most common complaint is diarrhoea. This can be caused simply by a change of diet, or more likely by the poor hygiene standards. Treatments such as Imodium or Lomotil are recommended as part of the medical kit, as are a few sachets of rehydrating salts, such as Dioralyte. More serious diarrhoea may need to be treated with antibiotics. If it persists, seek medical attention. I have never heard of any cases of amoebic dysentery, although the lack of hygiene would suggest this is a possibility.

Whilst Acute Mountain Sickness cannot be ruled out, it is very unlikely. However, mild symptoms of altitude sickness such as headaches, general listlessness and loss of appetite may occur. If these symptoms persist (particularly headaches) descend immediately. Other than this the heat causes problems to those unused to it, so ensure that plenty of liquids are consumed.

**Emergency Services**
There are no official rescue organisations serving the Atlas mountains. All CAF huts possess a stretcher, first aid box and manual (N.B. beware the fact that certain huts, e.g. Lepiney refuge, are normally locked). Assistance in fetching help is usually available since the mountains are heavily populated. Evacuation by mule is easy to arrange, if the patient is in a fit state to travel. In more serious cases evacuation by helicopter is possible (there is one stationed at Marrakech). The nearest telephones in the Toubkal region are at Oukaimeden and Asni, (lines were cut to Imlil at the time of writing but may now be restored). Contact police in the first instance.

**Maps and Where to Obtain Them**
A pleasant surprise for the visitor is that Morocco is well mapped and furthermore that the maps are not restricted to military use.

The whole of the Atlas and Anti-Atlas have been mapped at 1:100,000 scale, published in a series since 1970. In addition, the Toubkal region is covered by a 1:50,000 scale map, published in 1968.

These maps both suffer from a degree of inaccuracy and a lack of detail. The 1:100,000 series lacks many of the names of passes, peaks, and spot heights. It does, however, have relief and is easy to interpret. The 1:50,000 maps whilst obviously more detailed, are difficult to read as most contour heights are unmarked, and rocky areas are confusing. Nevertheless they are the best available and should be adequate for walking purposes. It is planned to map the whole of the Atlas in 1:50,000 scale.

The following is a list of the titles of maps which cover the areas in the guide:

Toubkal region: Jbel Toubkal (1:50,000), Oukaimeden-Toubkal (1:100,000). These 1:100,000 maps also cover the extreme western and southern corners of the Toubkal region - Amizmiz (W), Tizi-n'Test (SW), Taliwine (S).

Mgoun area: unfortunately the Mgoun massif overlaps the corners of 4 1:100,000 maps! They are - Azilal (NW), Zawyat Ahancal (NE), Qalaa't Mgouna (SE), Skoura (SW),

Telouat (Feuille no. NH 29 XXIII 2) links the Oukaimeden-Toubkal and Skoura maps, thus providing information for anyone wishing to undertake a traverse between the two regions.

Jebel Sahro: on the 1:100,000 series, Tazzarine covers the bulk of the region, whilst Boumalne (feuille no. NH 30 XIX 1) covers the northern fringes, including the important centre of Iknion. Ait Youl and the western fringes are on the Qalaa't Mgouna map (feuille no. NH 29 XXIV 2).

Mention should be made of the pre-war 1:20,000 maps of the Toubkal region, the result of French survey work. The original plan had been to map the whole of the region on this scale, but war intervened. The two maps which were completed are still far and away the best maps of the Toubkal area. Whilst having been unavailable for many years, the maps can be seen in the CAF refuges. Anyone wishing to produce copies of these maps would be assured of a good market.

In Britain Stanfords (12-13 Long Acre, London WC2) used to stock 1:50,000 maps of the Toubkal region, but now apparently no longer do so. It may be worth checking with them, however, since they can occasionally be acquired. They can also get the 1:100,000 Mgouen massif and Toubkal maps.

In Morocco the maps are supplied by a government agency, the Ministère de l'Agriculture et de la Reforme Agraire, (Division de la Carte) Rabat. They are available in Marrakech at the Hotel Ali, and sometimes in Imlil (for Toubkal region maps); price around £10.

## Dealing with the People

The Berbers of the Atlas mountains have a largely self-sufficient way of life, with little reliance on the outside world. A consequence of this is that most Berbers have very little money with which to buy luxuries or necessary tools. A European tourist therefore represents a big potential source of income to them. This is now the case in the Toubkal region and tourism plays a large part of the local economy. So, the Berbers invariably try to overcharge for whatever service or goods they provide the tourist with. It is important to bargain for everything. When passing through a village, one is constantly pestered by children asking for sweets and money. Adults ask for money, cigarettes and aspirin which, in the absence of medical facilities, serves as a universal panacea. Another situation the trekker commonly experiences is the invitiations to eat, or drink tea, only to be presented with a bill afterwards.

It would be wrong to dwell on the Berbers' bad points, there is much to be gained from meeting them. Outside of commercial transactions the Berbers are usually very friendly and well-mannered. Theft is rare and on trek possessions are safe in their hands. It is worth establishing what food is shared on trek as items such as coffee and jam are real luxuries and will be rapidly consumed otherwise.

Berbers are excellent linguists, besides their own unwritten language and Arabic many also speak French. Only a few, however, speak English.

Do not miss hearing some Berber music with its very African rhythm and complicated drumming. The singing takes the form of

*Muleteers making bread on trail*

call and response and the overall effect is an exciting, distinctive sound. There are opportunities to hear such singing at the 'Moussem' in the first week of September at Aroumd (a large festival in honour of Sidi (St.) Chamarouch).

Finally the Aid el-Kebir, or festival of the sheep, is an important celebration. Moslem rather than Berber, it celebrates Abraham's willingness to sacrifice Isaac and it lasts three days. On the first day each family slaughters a sheep or goat, after first dressing in white. Where it differs in the Atlas, however, is in what happens next. From the finest fresh goat skins, a costume is stitched together in preparation for the next day. The costumes are worn by the two most eligible young males in the village. They present a bizarre spectacle, as they run around the village, chasing everyone who emerges from their house. This game of hide and seek continues all day. On the evening of the second day the head male of each household tells the history of their family going back for generations. This oral tradition is believed to be pre-Islamic in origin.

## Mule Hire and Local Guides

## Mule Hire

The absence of supplies, the distance from roadheads and general lack of facilities necessitate carrying all equipment whilst on trek. By far the easiest way of doing this is to hire mules. As described in the introduction, the Atlas are criss-crossed with a network of mule trails. This, together with the low cost, make mule hire an attractive option.

The usual arrangement is that you hire the mule, the muleteer who accompanies it does not charge for his services. In the Toubkal area each mule has its own muleteer; in other areas a muleteer may look after two or three mules.

Rates are set by the government and are currently 75 Drh. per day. On top of this it is customary, if on a trek, to either provide food for the muleteers, or give them money to buy their own. Expect to pay around 30-40 Drh. per muleteer per day.

All rates should be negotiated beforehand, as should food arrangements for the muleteers. Frequently, unless otherwise agreed, the muleteers will arrive in camp foodless and expect to share your supplies. This obviously plays havoc with your planning.

At the end of each trek it is customary to give a "cadeau" equivalent to one day's wages to each muleteer (i.e. the cost of a day's mule hire). Tips are officially illegal in Morocco, hence the request is disguised as a gift.

The mules and muleteers move very fast over the ground; irrespective of your level of fitness, you would be hard pushed to keep up. Consequently they usually depart well after the trekkers. It is advisable to carry a packed lunch as on a typical day the mules will overtake you in the early afternoon. Mint tea will be brewing by the time you arrive.

## Local Guides

Undoubtedly on your arrival in Imlil you will be importuned by people offering their services as guides; they are unliklkey to be official mountain guides but will certainly have a knowledge of all the valleys and passes. However, with the aid of this book, it shouldn't be necessary to hire a guide. This is particularly true if you

*Berber muleteers encountered on the Tizi-n'Aguersioual*
*Amsakrou in the background*

are hiring mules - the muleteers will perform the function.

The official daily rate for a local guide is 200 Drh. Visitors to Jebel Sahro may wish to hire a guide. Beware of rogues, it is often difficult to tell in advance, but if in doubt never hire a guide who does not live in the area.

Anyone wishing to hire an official guide should contact the Moroccan Office de Tourisme in Marrakech, (Place Abd el-Moumen ben Ali, Guêliz).

*N.B.  Porters*

Up until June, or even later, many of the high passes (e.g. Tizi-n'Ouanoumss) are impassable by mule. In these circumstances it is necessary to hire porters. Each porter will carry *c.* 25 kilos. Rates are cheaper than mule hire but, obviously, porters can carry much less. This can be arranged in larger villages such as Imlil.

# PART THREE
## The Toubkal Region

## Introduction

This area, containing all the highest peaks, is by far the most popular region in the Atlas for walkers. The trek up to Toubkal and the Neltner hut is undertaken by several thousand visitors each year, of all nationalities. Travel beyond the narrow confines of the Mizane valley, however, and you are unlikely to meet more than one or two other trekkers.

Roughly speaking, the Toubkal area is bounded by the Tizi-n'Test to the west, and the Tizi-n'Tichka to the east. Most of the interest is concentrated in or around the central line of peaks from Ouanoukrim north-east to Annrhemer and Angour.

## Starting Points

The area is invariably approached from Marrakech, taking the Tizi-n'Test road as far as Asni. Asni has a garage, shops, telephone, and a postbox but is of little interest to visitors except for the Hotel Toubkal, a 4-star hotel with swimming pool just before the Imlil turnoff (open to non-residents, 25 Drh. to use pool). This makes a very pleasant break to the journey. There is also a hostel on the opposite side of the road. In spring when there is too much snow on the high peaks for walking, there is a very pleasant walk up on to the Kik plateau from Asni. This is botanically very interesting, and provides superb views of the main Atlas chain.

## The Mizane Valley: Imlil and Aroumd

This is far and away the most frequented of the bases for exploring the mountains.

## Imlil (1,740m)

A large village situated at the end of the motor road, 17 kms from Asni. As it is the standard approach route for those wishing to climb Toubkal it is well geared to supplying the trekkers' needs. There are

38

several shops selling drinks, tinned foods, sweets and biscuits. In addition there are a few very basic restaurants and the inevitable souvenir stalls. Of importance to the trekker, there is also a grocer selling a range of fresh fruit and vegetables. Shops here sell both the 1:50,000 and 1:100,000 scale maps of the area.

Adjoining the main square is the CAF refuge. This is a cut above any of the surrounding accommodation being spacious and comfortable, with a small garden. It is clean inside with a dining-room, kitchen (gas and all utensils), showers and bunk beds with foam mattresses. The Etoile du Toubkal provides decent accommodation for those not continuing to Aroumd.

1997 rates: as for other CAF huts, 40 Drh. per night + 3 Drh. compulsory charge for service.

Imlil is the best place to arrange mules for transporting baggage. Theoretically there are fixed rates for both mule and guide hire; in practice this never applies. If staying in the CAF refuge the warden will assist in finding mules. Otherwise it is an easy matter to find someone willing to provide a mule. Negotiations are best conducted over a cup of mint tea in a nearby café. Be prepared to haggle.

What you pay for is the mule, the muleteer's service is included in the price. If it seems unnecessary to have one muleteer per mule bear in mind that each mule is worth around £500, a considerable sum to a villager and an investment that must be cared for. By and large the mules are well looked after in the mountains.

1997 rates: expect to pay around 75 Drh. a day per mule. On top of this a 'cadeau' of one day's wages is expected by each muleteer. Remember that these prices are a guideline only, dependent upon your desire and ability to haggle. Remember also that when loading mules the Berbers will invariably try to supply one or two mules more than is necessary.

Hiring of guides, if desired, is also easy in Imlil.

Getting there: from Marrakech buses run at least 8 times a day to Asni. They depart from the Bab er Robb bus station (to Asni approx. 2 hours, c.20 Drh.). From Asni take a service bus (often a pick-up truck) to Imlil (17km). First few kms surfaced, then good dirt road to Imlil (1 hour, c.10-20 Drh.).

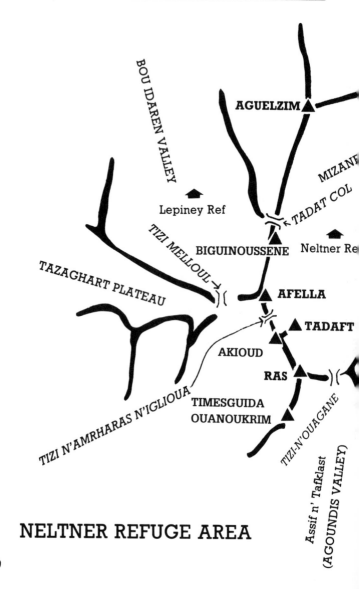

BOU IDAREN VALLEY

**AGUELZIM**

MIZANE

Lepiney Ref

TADAT COL

TIZI MELLOUL →

**BIGUINOUSSENE**

Neltner Re

TAZAGHART PLATEAU

**AFELLA**

▲ **TADAFT**

**AKIOUD**

**RAS**

TIZI N'AMRHARAS N'IGLIOUA

**TIMESGUIDA
OUANOUKRIM**

TIZI-N'OUAGANE

Assif n' Tafklast
(AGOUNDIS VALLEY)

# NELTNER REFUGE AREA

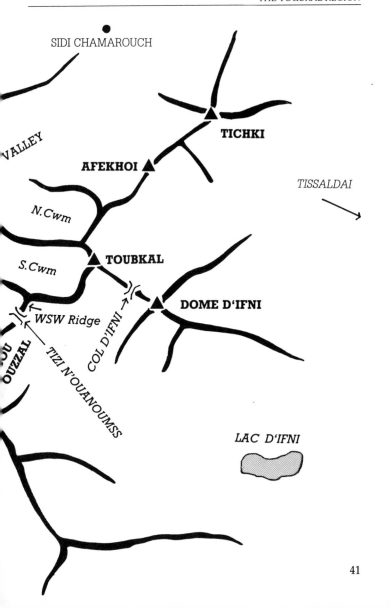

SIDI CHAMAROUCH

TICHKI

VALLEY

AFEKHOI

TISSALDAI

N.Cwm

S.Cwm

TOUBKAL

DOME D'IFNI

COL D'IFNI

WSW Ridge

OU OUZZAL

TIZI N'OUANOUMSS

LAC D'IFNI

**Aroumd (1,960m)** (also spelt Around, Aremd)

Situated 40 mins. walk up the valley from Imlil, it can also be reached by car via a rough track. Not visible from Imlil, Aroumd occupies the southern slopes of a huge landslip which is still virtually vegetation-free. An extensive area of terraced fields adjoins it.

Since the first edition of this guide was published, the accommodation in Aroumd has been considerably upgraded. There are now several small 'gîtes d'étape', around 32 Drh. per night, and hot showers are even available for 10 Drh. Mule hire can also be arranged here. The village serves as the base for a British trekking company.

## The Imenane Valley: Tacheddirt and Oukaimeden

The next valley east from the Mizane valley, separated from it by a long ridge which is crossed in several places by passes. A useful base for ascents of Angour and Annrhemer.

It is possible to drive into the upper Imenane valley from Imlil, although the road stops some way short of Tacheddirt, the highest village. A car left in the open here would be very vulnerable. The best approach, therefore, is either to walk over from Imlil or Aguersioual (q.v.). The latter approach, whilst longer, has the advantage of passing through the beautiful lower reaches of this valley.

### Tacheddirt (2,300m)

The only practical base in the valley. There is a CAF refuge here at the western end of the village, marked on 1:50,000 map. More basic than the Imlil refuge but with cooking facilities it sleeps 20. No shops in the village but bread and eggs usually available. Vegetables in season, possibly. Mule hire available.

### Oukaimeden (2,610m)

A small ski resort situated in a high basin NE of Imlil. It is rather too far north for serving as a base for climbing Toubkal, though ideal for ascending Angour and visiting the upper Ourika valley. Oukaimeden has a telephone and a road connection with Marrakech.

Being a ski resort it is very quiet in summer, with only a few local herders around. Mule hire is therefore not feasible. Throughout summer there are one or two local shops open, selling the usual tinned goods at more than usually exorbitant prices. In winter there are several hotels and restaurants open.

Open throughout the year is the CAF refuge. This is a large building with the appearance of a hotel. Inside this initial impression is reinforced, there is a bar room, games room, and even a bandstand! Additionally there are showers (not always hot), comfortable bedrooms and good cooking facilities. Very clean. No food is available, visitors must supply their own. 40 Drh. per night.

A much nicer alternative, in my view, is Chez Ju-Ju. This is a hotel/restaurant 100 yards further up the road. It is run by a French lady who has been here since just after the war. There is dormitory accommodation, with clean sheets, at a very reasonable charge, hot showers included. Breakfast, with expresso coffee, and best of all, French cuisine, a three-course meal is also available. It is also the only place in the mountains where alcohol is served. Beer is served ice-cold and is extremely welcome in mid-summer. Chez Ju-Ju is open all year round, except during the month of Ramadan.

Getting there: Oukaimeden is connected to Marrakech by road. This road (signposted in Marrakech) leads via the Ourika valley, with plenty of hairpins, to Oukaimeden. An alternative, if driving, is to continue towards Asni. A mile beyond Tahannaout turn L along a signposted road. This route is very scenic. There is also a dirt road connecting Asni with Oukaimeden, used mainly by mine trucks. There is a bus service from Marrakech in winter, but in summer it is necessary to hire a *grand taxi*. Hitching there is also easy, though occasionally slow.

## Peripheral Bases
### Setti Fadma

Situated in the Ourika valley, at the eastern edge of the region, it is seldom visited by walkers. This is a pity, as it is only two days walk from Tacheddirt and Oukaimeden, through lovely scenery.

Getting there: several buses, service taxis from Marrakech. It is also feasible to hitch; this is a popular destination for Moroccans.

Follow the S 513 as for Oukaimeden, continue along the main valley to Aghbalou (1,011m) where there is a smart French restaurant. Also good restaurant/hotel at Assgaour, 1 km before Setti Fadma, though this had in 1988 gone downhill somewhat. Road continues to Setti Fadma, which is like a bigger version of Imlil. There are several shops and small Moroccan restaurants selling tajine and brochettes etc. Mule hire possible.

The reason for Setti Fadma's popularity with locals is the cascades, beautiful waterfalls 30 mins. walk from the village. Well worth a visit. Setti Fadma also serves as a good base for ascending some of the outlying peaks (e.g. Meltsen and Yagour - see under relevant section). From Setti Fadma to Timichchi (q.v.) is 6-7 hours walking along the main Ourika valley.

## Amsouzart
An interesting alternative approach to the Toubkal massif from the S side. There are few facilities here, but several shops exist and mule hire is possible. Reached via dirt road which connects with the P32 Taroudant - Taliwine road. Good for access to Lac d'Ifni, Dome d'Ifni and Adrar n'Dern.

## Tizi-n'Test
On the N (Asni) side of the pass the village of Ijoukak provides a good base for the westernmost peaks of the region. It is at the lower end of the Agoundis valley which leads to the Tizi Melloul (q.v.). Mule hire possible, several shops, meals and rooms available. Several treks start or finish here. To gain the Agoundis valley it is possible to drive along a dirt track to the village of Taghbart from here.

## Mountain Refuges
People visiting the region often lack either the time or the desire to undertake a trek; the CAF refuges, however, make ideal bases for a short stay or for peak-bagging.

*Terracing, Amsakrou*

## Neltner Refuge (3,207m)

The most frequently used by far of all the mountain refuges. Its popularity is due largely to its situation at the very foot of Toubkal. It is open throughout most of the year, new snow making it inaccessible sometimes in winter. It sleeps 30, has cooking facilities and Coke and Fanta for sale. Since the first edition of this guide, the former hut warden, a great character known to most simply as "Haj", has retired, and the refuge is now run by his son.

Just below the Neltner hut is a level campsite. It is possible to stop here and use the hut facilities at a small charge.

### Imlil to Neltner Refuge

The standard approach, and the best-used path in the Atlas. From Imlil take the main track heading up from the square. Follow this out of the village, where it turns R, then back L. Where it makes a second sharp turn R by a pink house take the footpath which leads straight on.

Continue along the path through fields to a watercourse, passing a house on L. Stay in this line for 100 metres or so beyond the house until the path starts to switchback. Up this to reach the motorable dirt road to Aroumd. Take this, past the Café Lac d'Ifni (a new building opposite the main village of Aroumd).

Stay on this track, which enters the broad valley base ahead (40 mins.). It leads to the head of the field system, where an obvious track heads L up the valley side, passing a huge boulder and a few walnut trees. Go past these to where the track levels out a little. It leads in *c.*2 hours 30 mins. to a ford in the stream just below a large white-painted boulder. The boulder marks the shrine, or *marabout,* of Sidi Chamarouch (2,340m) and contains a small mosque. It is a popular place of local pilgrimage as the source which emerges from the rocks here is reputed to have healing powers. The waters are meant to be especially good in curing leg ailments. How true it is I don't know, but I have seen someone being helped unsteadily down from here by his two friends. When I asked about this his friends told me that he had been carried up there as a cripple, but now, after three days, he was able to walk.

*Ilfoulou, Tessaout Valley*

*Crossing the "Neve Permanent" Beneath the Tazaghart cliffs*
*on the way to Tizi Melloul. Early September*

*Sidi Chamarouch*

Across the stream from the shrine, and reached by a small footbridge, is a collection of small shops selling trinkets, chocolate and the ubiquitous tins of sardines. Prices here are some of the most extortionate I've encountered in Morocco.

From Sidi Chamarouch take the steep zig-zags on the RH side (true L bank) to emerge onto an easy-angled path leading up the valley.Toubkal is the huge bulk on the opposite bank. An hour or so after Sidi Chamarouch the Tadat pinnacle (q.v.) appears conspicuously on the skyline ahead. The Neltner hut eventually emerges into view, 20 mins. before arrival there (4 hours 30 mins. from Imlil).

## Lepiney Refuge (3,000m)

Remotely situated in the upper Azzaden valley this is a small hut which receives few visitors. It is delightfully situated near a waterfall. The view outside the hut is completely dominated by the cliffs of the Tazaghart plateau, which at 650m are the biggest in the area. The hut sleeps 20 and has gas stoves but few cooking utensils - take pans etc. Snow conditions may make the refuge inaccessible in winter and in summer it is kept locked when unoccupied. The warden lives in the first large village down the valley, Tizi Oussem. If travelling to the hut with muleteers make sure they alert the warden by sending someone ahead. If backpacking there is little alternative to making the detour via Tizi Oussem to fetch the warden. This may explain why it is so rarely visited!

## Imlil to Lepiney Refuge

An early start is advisable. From Imlil head up the main track from the square. After 250m take a path on R which heads towards a collection of houses. Pass these and continue heading up the valley towards the Tizi Mzik. A steep mule trail leads in 1 hour 30 mins. to the col (2,485m). (This point can be reached from Aroumd by following the motor road back towards Imlil as far as the first hairpin. A faint track leads off across the L hillside to join up with the main mule trail a few hundred metres below the col.)

From here take the path which contours L across the hillside. After a while the village of Tizi Oussem comes into view below. Where the path appears to split, crossing a steep patch of scree, take the lower junction. Shortly after this the path becomes indistinct whilst passing through juniper trees. Don't worry if you seem to be losing too much height. The path bends L to skirt a broad gully (the path down to the valley floor is now obvious). Keep contouring and soon the tongue of debris on which Azib Tamsoult is built appears, followed by the azib itself. Cross the stream - a good lunch spot (3 hours from Imlil).

From the stream head up L and enter the azib on its LH side. This is a good example of a Berber azib, utilising the available rocks with fences constructed of massive branches. The tin building is marked on the map as a refuge, though heaven knows what function it performs.

Continue up through the village to the main river-bed above. The path becomes indistinct again here as it winds its way across frequently wet ground towards the narrows ahead. Cross to the L bank where a good mule track leads in zig-zags up past some beautiful waterfalls to emerge into a high basin ahead. Continue

*The endless screes in the ascent of Toubkal via the S. Cwm.*
*The ridge in the background is Biguinoussene, with the Tadat pinnacle*
*clearly visible. The descent from Tadat col takes the obvious scree gully*
*just to the right of Tadat pinnacle*

along the mule track until the refuge is reached, (7-8 hours from Imlil).

## Excursions from the Neltner Refuge

Toubkal and most of the other highest peaks of the Atlas encircle the head of this valley. All can be done in a day from the hut.

## Jebel Toubkal (4,167m)

The highest mountain in North Africa, the goal of countless visitors who would never normally go near a mountain. Most who make the ascent hate it; I love it. True the screes are interminable, but at least they are reasonably firm underfoot. Toubkal has several satellite peaks which are described later.

The bulk of ascents of Toubkal are made via the S Cwm route, which starts directly behind the Neltner refuge.

*Toubkal summit. In the background, the twin summits of
Ouanoukrim - Timesguida (4088m.) on the L.
Ras (4083m.) on the R.*

## Toubkal via S Cwm

From the Neltner hut take the path past the rain gauge (with
helpful sign on it!) for 50m or so, to where a path leads L to drop
down to the river. Cross the river, scramble up the other banks to
a good track which leads to the foot of the first screes. Starting from
the RH side cross diagonally to boulders and bed-rock. From here
head up the bed of the cwm on boulders and a scree-covered path to
large boulders seen on the skyline from the hut (1 hour).

Continue on a well-defined path into the main cwm. There are
two alternatives here: L and up horrible long scree slope to N side
of the summit or, much better, head R up a steep scree to an easy-
angled scree leading to the Tizi-n'Toubkal (3,940m, 2 hours 15
mins.). From here follow the ridge and the path just below the ridge
to arrive at the summit, (3 hours 15 mins.).

The summit is adorned with a large, iron, pyramidal structure.
There are excellent views, heat haze permitting, of surrounding
peaks: to S Jebel Siroua, to SE Jebel Sahro. (The nearby conical red

*The Dome d'Ifni seen from just below Toubkal summit*

peak to the SE connected to Toubkal is the Dome d'Ifni, or Ouimli-
lene (3,876m), not really feasible from Toubkal.) The small stone
shelters on the summit of Toubkal are for bivvying, if you have a
good sleeping bag, (well worthwhile to enjoy the dawn).

Descent: the same way down, 1 hour 30mins.-2 hours 30mins.
depending on one's ability and aptitude for scree running.

## Toubkal via N Cwm

This is the next big cwm down the valley from the S cwm. The scree
is not as bad as on the normal route. Makes a good combination with
the S cwm route.

From the refuge follow the trail down towards Sidi Chamarouch
for a few hundred metres, then cross the river before the N cwm
entrance. There is a faint track which leads diagonally across the
lower screes into the cwm proper. Head up on R of the cwm bed to
enter this shortly before it bends round and steepens. Ascend the
rock steps which lead to a gap on the L, up this and continue R
towards the main ridge at a col. Follow this to reach the summit.
(3hrs.30mins-4hrs.).

## Toubkal via Ouanoumss Ridge

This classic route involves actual climbing and is unsuitable for walkers. It is described here for those who feel capable of tackling it. It is one of the finest expeditions of its type in the Atlas. Equivalent to Alpine grade D.

From the Neltner refuge take the main path leading up the valley. After *c.*45mins. you reach a stony plain dotted with large boulders. At the end of this plain cross the river, then head up the screes on a faint zig-zag path to reach the obvious gap - the Tizi-n'Ouanoumss (3,664m, 1hr.30mins.-2hrs. see p.68).

From the col scramble up the scree to the base of the crag proper. Climb this to reach a chimney which skirts a large pinnacle on R. This leads to the ridge crest, which is followed to a small col. Climb the face above, trending R, to reach a scree slope. Abseil down into the gap ahead. Ascend the crack (or more easily, go L to reach a loose gully) to arrive on the crest. Follow this to the final real obstacle, a wall which is ascended via a chimney to reach an easier ridge. This leads to a shoulder. Continue along the ridge, much easier now, to a large, rocky eminence (4,020m) just before the Tizi-n'Toubkal (4hrs. from Tizi-n'Ouanoumss). Continue via the normal route to the summit (6hrs.-6hrs.30mins.).

## Satellite Peaks of Toubkal

Tibherine (4,010m) can be combined with an ascent of Toubkal. From the gap beyond the rock steps, contour away from the Toubkal summit to reach a col on the main ridge descending from Toubkal NE. Ascend over rocks to the summit, which has the remains of an aircraft adorning it (20mins.).

Imousser (3,890m) is just as close. From the col on the main ridge leading up to the Toubkal summit climb easily up the ridge opposite. At the breach in the ridge drop down to the L to regain the ridge beyond the difficulties. Continue along this, airily, to the summit (25-30mins.).

## Ouanoukrim (4,088m)

A superb mountain, the second highest in the Atlas and one of the most enjoyable. Not to be missed. It consists of two summits; the N

*Nearing the Tizi-n'Ouagane, Upper Mizane Valley.*
*Behind the Biguinoussene ridge leading to Aguelzim*

summit (4,083m) known as Ras, and the slightly higher S summit, Timesguida (4,088m). The two tops are separated by an easy scree-field.

## Ouanoukrim via E Ridge

The normal ascent route, it takes the short ridge descending to the Tizi-n'Ouagane.

From the Neltner hut follow the path as for Tizi-n'Ouanoumss to where it crosses the stream, at the end of the plain (45-50mins.). Instead of crossing keep on the R side of the stream and walk up a stony track (steeply at first). This leads into a higher basin (1hr.05 mins.) that has snow patches even in late summer. The Tizi-n'Ouagane lies straight ahead.

The next section, up the col, is steep and tiring. In ascent it is probably best to take the RH side, crossing the stream coming in from the R, up to the bedrock. Walk diagonally across, travel over a boulder field low down and rejoin the main path to col (2hrs.).

Up from the col the route takes the crested ridge. Skirt the R side of the prominent 20ft twin fangs of rock (10mins. from the col). Walk straight up the crest of the rock ridge (easier than it looks) to reach a mule-width track after 200 feet or so. Head R into a gully, walk up, it is a short way to rejoin the crest which you follow for a few feet. The angle soon starts to relent until one finds oneself on an easy-angled scree slope, the summit scree field, (40mins. 2hrs.40 mins. from the refuge). On the previous section the secret is to keep R of the main crest if in doubt at any stage. **N.B.** Make a note of the exit point onto the summit scree field for descending; it is not that easy to find if there are no cairns.

Continue just L of the crest on the R overlooking Akioud, then up screes to reach the summit of the N peak, Ras (4,083m, 3hrs.). Fine views of the Toubkal massif. From here it is 20-25mins. to the S summit. On descent from the S summit aim for Angour initially (i.e. NE) and avoid dropping down too far R. Rejoin the ascent route just above rock bands. Descent: 50mins. to the col, 2-2hrs.30mins. back to the refuge.

## Ouanoukrim via NW Ridge

Not as enjoyable as the normal ascent (there is a lot of scree) although the two can be combined. As for the normal route as far as the higher basin (1hr.05mins.). Head into the obvious side valley, across some unpleasant ground, to reach the col ahead (Tizi-n'Bou Imrhaz, 3,875m, 2hrs.30mins.-3hrs.).

From here, follow the ridge directly to the N summit. Loose in places, but easy scrambling (1hr. from the col, 3hrs.30mins-4hrs. in total).

## Bou Ouzzal (3,860m)

A buttressed ridge between the Tizi-n'Ouanoumss and the Tizi-n'Ouagane (q.v.). A short but worthwhile expedition in its own right combined with an ascent of Ouanoukrim.

There are four tops, each of which can be reached with varying degrees of difficulty. The ridge direct involves climbing, but difficulties can be avoided by scrambling detours.

## Akioud (4,010m)

A fine rocky peak which presents another worthwhile objective from the Neltner hut. It is the next peak north from Ouanoukrim, the two being separated by the Tizi-n'Bou Imrhaz.

There are two commonly used routes, but only one easy route for walkers (via NNW ridge).

## Akioud via NNW Ridge

From the Neltner hut a very prominent, deep valley descends to the R of Akioud. The first part of the route tackles this.

From the refuge as for the Tizi-n'Ouanoumss route until the level plain just beyond the low, yellow crags is reached (40-45mins.). Then head R up into the valley, continue to reach the col. This is the Tizi-n'Amrharas n'Iglioua (3,815m, 2hrs.30mins-3hrs.), a popular route over to Tazaghart and the Lepiney refuge.

From the col skirt R (westwards) to avoid a rock step, then continue easily to the N summit (40mins. from the col). This is the highest of the 3 main tops of Akioud.

Descend via the same route.

## Akioud from the Tizi-n'Bou Imrhaz

A tiring route over loose scree, its sole merit is in providing a means of traversing Akioud and Ouanoukrim.

Follow the Ouanoukrim NW ridge route as far as the Tizi-n'Bou Imrhaz, (2hrs.30mins.-3hrs.). From here skirt round the base of the wall on the R (east) side, cross the steep scree leading to the col between Akioud and Tadaft. At the col ascend the gully on R (loose and unpleasant) to emerge on the main Akioud ridge (between the middle top and the higher N summit). Scramble on good rock to the N summit (1hr.30mins.-1hr.45mins. from col, 4hrs.-5hrs.30mins. total).

## Tadaft (*c.*3,905m)

This is an impressive and much sought-after pinnacle situated on a ridge running from Akioud toward the Mizane valley. Unfortunately it is the area's equivalent of the 'inaccessible pinnacle', beyond the scope of walkers.

### Afella (4,015m)

Another popular summit, best reached from the Tizi Melloul. (see p.67). The summit consists of two tops separated by a broad saddle.

From the refuge as for Akioud normal route to the Tizi-n'Amrharas N'Iglioua, (3,815m, 2hrs.30mins-3hrs.). Descend the far side for a short distance until it is possible to traverse R and round the flank until the Tizi Melloul comes into view. Make for the Tizi Melloul, or the broad spur above it on R. From Tizi Melloul, Afella is a short ascent following the broad spur SE (20-25mins. from Tizi Melloul, 3hrs.45mins-4hrs.15mins. total).

### Tazaghart Plateau (3,984m)

This huge weird plateau dominates the west side of the Toubkal area. It is linked by the Tizi Melloul to the other mountains in the range. On the top it is flat enough to land an aircraft. The summit plateau extends for many acres, a stony, desolate place devoid of vegetation. There is little to see up here, but the extraordinary nature of the place makes it an unforgettable experience. There is a shrine somewhere on the plateau which dates back centuries, but I have yet to find it. One of the least-frequented of the peaks in this region.

From Tizi Melloul follow the easy stepped ridge, the scree and path (faint in places) to the edge of the summit plateau. The cairn ahead marks the highest point (20-25mins. from col).

### Biguinoussene (3,990m)

North of Afella the bounding ridge of the upper Mizane valley continues as a jagged crest. As a whole it is known as Biguinoussene.

The highest point of this ridge is towards the N end; the southern sections of the ridge are known as the Clochetons.

### Biguinoussene from Tizi-n'Tadat

Outside the Neltner refuge a mule track leads straight out from the door towards the scree, then traverses R across the hillside. Follow this to where it arrives at a big gully/rift which leads right up to the main ridge (15mins.). Walk up the gully bed until it becomes a scramble. Then head out of the bed up steep rock and scree slopes. These lead after 1hr. approx. to a horizontal track, well defined. (This is the descent route described as an alternative from Lepiney refuge, p.77).

Follow the track back towards the gully, below a low rockface. Gain a well constructed track which leads up to the base of the main scree run, then up to the Tizi-n'Tadat. Fight your way up this (utter misery guaranteed) to reach an abrupt saddle, the Tizi-n'Tadat. (*c*.3,725m, 2hrs.30mins.). The prominent pinnacle is **Tadat (*c*.3,755m)**. The easiest route of ascent is on the shorter S side, British V Diff. in grade, 50ft.

Skirt round the base of (or ascend) Tadat and follow the crest of the ridge, without difficulty, to the summit (40mins., 3hrs.10mins. from hut).

## Continuation from Biguinoussene (The Clochetons)

This involves difficult scrambling/easy climbing in exposed positions. A rope is useful, particularly if an *integràle* ascent is made.

From the summit of Biguinoussene continue along the crest until it begins to dip steeply. Climb down to above a tower. Turn the tower on the R, and continue enjoyably along an exposed crest to reach a brèche where the rock ends. Ahead are the Clochetons. Keep on the R side, climb over scree ledges to reach a gap in the Clochetons ridge.

From here a delightful ridge leads to the northern Clocheton: hard scrambling, with some awkward moves. Return along same route to the gap.

From the gap, a horizontal traverse line leads on the R (W) side of the Clochetons to a gap beyond the southernmost Clocheton. Harder variations enable the summits of the Clochetons themselves to be attained (3hrs. from Biguinoussene, slightly faster in return direction).

## Aguelzim (3,650m)

This is the continuation ridge N from Tizi-n'Tadat which can be followed all the way back to Imlil. An interesting alternative to the normal Sidi Chamarouch route.

From the Tizi-n'Tadat (q.v.) follow the ridge, with easy scrambling, to where it overlooks the lower Mizane valley. Continue down to a col - the Tizi-n'Tizikert. From here a path leads down on the R to emerge in the valley above Aroumd. Alternatively keep on the ridge, over Adrar el Hajj (3,129m, called Adrar Adj on 1:100,000 maps) to reach the Tizi Mzik (q.v.). Descend this to Imlil.

## The Complete Circuit

It is possible to stay on the ridge crest right the way round from Toubkal to Ouanoukrim etc. back to Imlil. This would take several days. Either bivvy en route, or descend to the Neltner hut each evening.

For the sake of completeness the traverse should be started by heading L from Sidi Chamarouch to the Tizi-n'Tarharat, then moving on to Toubkal via Tichki (3,627m) and Afekhoi (3,751m).

## Toubkal from Sidi Chamarouch via Tichki and Afekhoi

From Sidi Chamarouch, descend for 5 minutes to cross the stream via the ford below the village. (The footbridge is for the use of Muslim pilgrims to the shrine only.) Head back upstream to gain the Tizi-n'Tarharat track, which zig-zags up to the broad saddle of the Tizi-n'Tarharat (3,456m, 3hrs.30mins.).

Take the N ridge, easy scrambling, which leads to the summit of Tichki (1hr.30mins. from col. N.B. on 1:100,000 map, height is given as 3,753m). The ridge leads past a series of towers, avoided on either side, to a col, the Tizi-n'Tichki. Continue along the ridge to reach Afekhoi (3,751m, 3,755m on 1:100,000 maps). The main ridge continues from here to Toubkal.

The section of the circuit most frequently walked from the Neltner refuge is from Ouanoukrim to Tizi-n'Tadat. This can be done in a long day, returning to the hut. A classic excursion.

## Excursions from the Lepiney Refuge

This is the best base for ascending Tazaghart and Afella, but otherwise there is not a great deal to offer the walker; it is primarily a climber's hut. Tazaghart and Afella are ascended from the Tizi Melloul (q.v.).

## Excursions from Tacheddirt

### Angour (3,616m)
(See Excursions from Oukaimeden p.63 for further routes and description.) From Tacheddirt it is possible to scramble directly to the Grouden col and the West ridge (q.v.). Unpleasant, and rarely done. A longer but preferable approach is via the Tizi-n'Ou Addi. Follow the path above Tacheddirt to Tizi-n'Ouadi (2hrs.30mins., see p.79). From here traverse across N slopes to gain the Grouden col.

### Angour via E Ridge
A delightful, airy ridge with a few awkward scrambling sections. From Tacheddirt head up the valley on a prominent mule track (zig-zags in the upper part) to the Tizi-n'Tacheddirt (3,230m, 2hrs.30mins.). At the col ascend directly up the slope to the N via what appears to be a weakness in the rock slabs. Easy scrambling leads to a rocky ridge looking northwards out over the Tissi plateau.

Follow this ridge W, either along the crest itself or just on the RH side, until the last, deepest notch before a rocky slab. 15 feet to the R, down from the col, there is a little rock gully. Go up this for 5 feet, traverse R for 100 feet to easier slabs and scree up to a level, grassy ridge. Head R to the main ridge, follow this to the lower S summit. The further N summit (3,616m) is best climbed from the gap on its RH side via rocky ledges, (4hrs.30mins.-5hrs.). Descent - 3 hours.

### Annrhemer (3,892m)
A challenging peak with no easy routes; all involve scrambling at the very least. The only route feasible for experienced walkers is:

### Annrhemer W Ridge from Tizi-n'Tacheddirt
As for Angour E ridge to the Tizi-n'Tacheddirt (2hrs.30mins.). Now head S to the rock outcrop. Easy ground to the L leads back to the main ridge. Continue in this line, avoiding rock outcrops on the L, to follow the ridge just L of the crest.

Where this fades, take a parallel ridge to the L which leads to a fang of rock. Now head past this to reach a prominent col, the Tizi-n'Tigourzatine (3,680m, 2hrs. from the col.).

Follow the ridge to the L of the col, on its RH side. This leads up to the slightly lower W summit. The ridge between here and the main summit is superb - airy and interesting. It has been likened to the Cuillin ridge. Along its crest are some outcrops of lovely rough, red granite, the best rock in the area. The scrambling is quite easy throughout. The main summit is reached after 3hrs.30mins. from Tizi-n'Tacheddirt, 6hrs. total.

Descent - the same route in reverse.

## Annrhemer via NE Ridge

Not for walkers since this route involves some easy climbing. Care is required in finding the easiest route, if undue difficulties are to be avoided. A description is included as an ascent of this, combined with a descent of the previous route (an easier descent), provides far and away the best traverse of the mountain. As the majority of the route is on the N side of the ridge, there is often a fair amount of snow around, even in mid-summer.

From the Tizi-n'Tacheddirt traverse R (eastwards) beneath the N face of Annrhemer to reach a large gully. Ascend this (unpleasant) to where an obvious big scree-fan comes in from the R. Ascend this to gain the ridge proper at a small gap.

From the gap follow the crest to where it abuts against a prominent steep step. This is avoided by dropping down R (N) to reach a slender weakness which leads up to a recess. From here regain the ridge, follow it to a gap. Descend down to the R of the gap to enter the gully just below it. Cross this to gain a rake which leads airily back up to the crest and over further steep ground to a lessening of angle and difficulty. Continue to the summit, mainly on the R side of the ridge.

## Bou Iguenouane (3,882m)

Compared with Angour and Annrhemer this mountain is lacking in appeal. The scree is particularly tiresome.

## Bou Iguenouane via WSW Ridge

From Tacheddirt descend from the village and climb up to the road on the opposite side of the valley. (This can be reached by following the road right round from Tacheddirt - longer but easier.) From the obvious spring at the start of the irrigation channel a deep valley rises ahead, trending up to the L. Follow it, over solid rocks at first, to encounter looser ground and eventually a long scree ascent to the Tizi Likemt (3,540m, 3hrs.30mins.).

From the col take the ridge on the L to reach a saddle. The ridge becomes narrower. The pinnacles ahead are avoided by contouring their base on the R (S) side. Rejoin the main ridge at a gap, follow the rocky crest to the summit (5hrs.30mins. total).

Descent - by same route.

## Aksoual (3,912m) & Tamadôt (3,842m)

These twin summits are separated by another highly enjoyable ridge, with easy scrambling. Unfortunately getting there is not so enjoyable. N.B. On 1:100,000 map the peak names are written in the wrong places.

In view of the length of the normal route, described below, it is worth considering a bivouac on the Tizi Likemt. This is especially true if the continuation to Tamadôt is intended.

## The ENE Ridge

As for previous route to Tizi-n'Likemt (3,540m, 3hrs.30mins.). Follow the ridge on the R, easily, over small knolls to where it narrows. Continue along this ridge to reach a col. The ridge leads, with excursions L to avoid difficulties, to the summit of Aksoual (3hrs. from Tizi Likemt, 6hrs.30mins. total).

Time permitting, the continuation ridge to Tamadôt is a must. From the summit of Aksoual descend the ridge, keeping slightly L (S). Reach a col in *c.*30mins. From here the pinnacled ridge ahead involves rock-climbing. To avoid this descend to the R, on the N side, and follow a good ledge beneath the pinnacles to reach a point between the 2 main tops of Tamadôt (1hr. from Aksoual, similar time in reverse).

## Aourirt n'Ouassif (2,724m)

As seen from Tacheddirt, this is the shapely conical peak just

*Angour from the summit of Jbel Oukaimeden.*
*To l. of summit, the Itbir Col. Skyline ridge to R. of summit is W. ridge.*
*Behind ,Iguenouane Anrhemmer and part of Bou Iguenouane on R.*

beyond the Tizi-n'Tamatert. It is a day's walk from Tacheddirt or Imlil and can be done as an addition to the walk between the two.

Take the motor road as far as the Tizi n'Tamatert (2,279m, q.v., 2hrs.). From the col ascend the ridge (steeply) to the false summit - the true summit is further W along the ridge (1hr.30mins. from the col.).

## Excursions from Oukaimeden

### Jbel Oukaimeden (3,263m)
This offers potentially the easiest ascent in the Atlas - there is a chair-lift to the top! However it only operates occasionally in the summer.

Despite this unsightly intrusion Jbel Oukaimeden makes an excellent short day, or afternoon walk, and has particularly fine views.

62

*Azib at Oukaimeden. Angour in the background*

From Chez Ju-Ju take the Tizi-n'Ou Addi road (leading to the ski-station) up the valley for 50 yards. Head across the plain, passing houses, to reach the base of the N ridge proper (20mins.). Follow the crest of the ridge, steeply, past an abandoned ski-station, to the easing of angle and the summit ski-station (1hr.45mins.).

Angour is seen clearly from here, and there is a fine view of the Toubkal range to the south.

## Angour (3,616m)

A magnificent mountain, one of the finest in the Atlas. It dominates the view SE from Oukaimeden. As seen from here the skyline ridge to the R of the summit is the classic west ridge. The Lakeland pioneer Bentley Beetham climbed the south face back in 1927.

The dominant feature of Angour is the large Tissi plateau which forms the eastern half of the mountain. Unlike the Tazaghart plateau it is low enough for the Berbers to graze sheep and goats on.

Climbing the west ridge, or the easier N gully route, from Oukaimeden involves scrambling. They are not therefore suitable

*Angour*

routes for the inexperienced.

For other routes on Angour see walks from Tacheddirt (p.60).

## Angour via W Ridge

From Chez Ju-Ju take the Tizi-n'Ou Addi (q.v.) road as far as the roadhead. Where the main path heads off, up the side of the valley, continue straight along the valley floor. Ahead and slightly L is an obvious col on the skyline, this is sometimes known as the Grouden col (3,090m). There is no real track up to this col, but ascend the R side of the cwm, keeping well to the R to avoid rock outcrops. Arrive at col (1hr.20mins.).

From the col the ridge is initially broad. Go along it, keeping to the L of the craggy section, to arrive below the sharp crest of the ridge. Follow the obvious grassy ledges to a flat ledge beneath a crag. Skirt this by going R and scrambling up a weakness to regain the ridge crest. Take the easiest line along this ridge, to where it broadens, and continue to a notch. Ascend the chimney for a few feet until it is possible to move L on easier ground which leads to a rocky slope. From here pass a step on the R and continue along the ridge crest. This is very narrow and exhilarating, but most of the difficulties can be avoided by detours L or R.

At the end of the ridge drop down a short way to a saddle. Head L to gain the edge of the summit plateau. Continue to arrive at the lower south summit. The main north summit is reached by descending into the gap and climbing up across rock ledges to gain the top (3,616m 4hrs-4hrs.30mins. from Oukaimeden).

Descent - either return by the same route, or reverse the north gully route (quicker but not as pleasant).

## Angour via N Gully

Whilst constituting the easiest means of ascent from Oukaimeden, it nevertheless contains some exposed passages and steep scrambling.

From Chez Ju-Ju take the Tizi-n'Ou Addi road, as for the previous route, to the roadhead (45mins.).

From Angour's impressive N buttress an obvious col can be seen at the base, this is the Tizi-n'Itbir (3,288m, clearly marked on maps). To reach this follow the valley which leads towards it. Take the zig-zag track to the col (1hr.30mins.).

Go up the scree to the open gully on the R of the N buttress. Ascend this, taking the easiest line (skirt rock pitches on the R). Continue up the gully bed until a breach in the main buttress can be seen to the L. Aim for this. At the gap an exciting path takes the horizontal ledge across the face. An easy path with terrific views, which leads into another gully that demarcates the N buttress on its eastern side. It can be reached from below (tiring, not recommended). Ascend this easily to the summit plateau. From the gap ascend the N summit as for the previous route (4hrs.).

Descent - same route.

## Other Points of Interest in Oukaimeden

A walk up to the radio-mast and observation platform gives good views (20mins.)

Oukaimeden is famous for its prehistoric rock-carvings. I have wasted many an hour searching for these things. Supposedly there is a map in the CAF refuge showing their whereabouts, but I haven't been able to find that either. Beyond the lake a local showed me a few insignificant marks on a rock one day. He said they represented a fish, although the similarity escaped me. Anyway, if you fancy searching, good luck to you!

## A Circuit of the Toubkal Region

This circuit, designed to be fitted into a two-week holiday from Britain, takes in most of the highlights of the region. Numerous variations are possible.

*Day 1    Imlil - Lepiney Refuge*

From Imlil follow the route over the Tizi Mzik to the Lepiney refuge (3,000m) as for p.49 (6-7hrs.).

*Day 2    Lepiney Refuge via Tizi Melloul to Neltner Refuge*

A fine day's walking through outstanding mountain landscape. There is the option of ascending Afella or the Tazaghart plateau.

From the refuge take the path leading up the valley on the L side of the stream bed past the waterfall. Cross the stream 100 yards beyond (ill-defined). Head over rough ground and make for the toe of a prominent snow-field (marked Névé Permanent on map).

The next section presents the greatest problems on the ascent (and in reverse) with awkward, though solid, scrambling. Harder if wet. A rope might be useful as a handrail/security.

Scramble up the gully bed, keeping to the L of the stream, to arrive at the lower rim of a huge cwm (1hr.40mins.). The cwm curves round to the R to Tizi Melloul (out of sight). Straight ahead are the Clochetons, with a couple of huge, prominent caves just above the scree at their base.

Follow the bed of the cwm easily to where it turns R and steepens. Tizi Melloul is straight ahead. Expect snowpatches even in autumn. Take the easiest line (mainly on R) up boulders to the col. Arrive slightly R of the lowest point of the col, skirting snowpatches (3,875m, 3hrs.15mins.).

Tazaghart (see p.57) is an easy ascent from this col. Follow the easy stepped ridge R (scree and a faint path in places) to arrive on the edge of the plateau. The prominent cairn just ahead marks the highest point (3,970m, 20mins. from the col). Descend by the same route to the col (15-20mins).

Afella (4,015m) is a slightly longer alternative from the col. Follow the obvious broad ridge to the E to arrive at a saddle between the two tops - the N top is slightly higher (30-35mins. from the col).

At the col the route skirts round the prominent spur of Afella ahead on the L. (Ascent of Afella from Neltner hut in reverse.) Contour round to the L, descending slightly, to turn this spur and ascend to the Tizi-n'Amrharas n'Iglioua (q.v.). 1hr.30mins. from Tizi Melloul.

Drop down the screes on the other side, keeping to the R side of the deep valley, to emerge in the upper Mizane valley at the level plain before the Tizi-n'Ouanoumss turn-off. Follow the main path down to the Neltner refuge (3hrs.30mins. from Tizi Melloul, 6hrs.45mins. from Lepiney refuge).

*Day 3    Neltner Refuge*
An opportunity to ascend Toubkal (q.v.) or one of the other peaks here (see Neltner refuge excursion notes, p.50).

*Day 4    Neltner Refuge via Tizi-n'Ouanoumss to Lac d'Ifni*
Take the good path from the hut which heads up the valley. Stay on the R bank of the stream. After 30mins. pass beneath yellow crags on the R (path a little indistinct here). The Tizi-n'Ouanoumss is the next prominent notch in the L valley wall after Toubkal S cwm.

The path soon becomes clear again as it winds its way through rock outcrops. After 45mins. reach a stony plain dotted with several large boulders. Cross this to its end, then cross the river. (The path to Tizi n'Ouagane and Ouanoukrim carries on along the R bank here.) Work your way up the scree slopes, keeping as close as possible to existing tracks, to reach the col (3,664m, 1hr.30mins.-2hrs.). The lake is visible from here - it is not visible during the descent.

The descent from the col to Lac d'Ifni is one of the longest in the Atlas, being fully 1,500m, or 5,000ft. Fortunately it is on a reasonable path which can, however, often be faint or eroded in the early season. Descend this path, which is through impressive rock scenery, to enter an area of huge boulders. The path winds its way through these to emerge onto a desolate alluvial plain. The lake is 30mins. further on. Aim for the L bank (N side) of the lake. Following this path round you find a campsite, with a few dry-stone walls for shelter, slightly beyond half-way down the lake.

Seen at close quarters the scummy appearance of the lake does not serve to make it inviting. However, I know plenty of people who have swum here with no ill effects. Besides, the lake is the only source of drinking water!

The bands around the water's edge are the result of attempts to regulate the inflow. Trout are rumoured to be found in this, the only lake of its kind on the southern side of the Atlas.

For all its proximity to the lake the campsite is still a bleak place, and very exposed to the wind. You may wish to continue for another hour or so to Imhilene, the first of the villages in the Tifnoute valley below. (See next day's route notes.)

## Day 5   Lac d'Ifni - Amsouzart - Tissaldai

Continue from the campsite to reach the end of the lake. As the path climbs you realise that the Lac d'Ifni is a lake without any outflow. At the top of the rise the path follows the edge of the steep valley side. The low mounds which block the eastern end of the lake are probably not glacial in origin, but fluvial.

Descend into the Tifnoute valley, and the first village, Imhilene, and continue past walnut groves down the valley. There is a choice of paths, on either side of the valley, both lead to Amsouzart (q.v.) where there are several shops. There is even one shop with a fridge here. The road has brought electricity with it and you can telephone here in case of emergency.

From Amsouzart another valley leads north into the mountains. This is the Tissaldai valley and it provides a delightful walk for the next part of the route. It is very fertile and in autumn there is plenty of fresh fruit to be had. Take the path which leads N from Amsouzart, on the RH side of the valley initially. At the narrows just beyond Timzakine keep on the R bank and pass through Tagadirt. Skirt round the spur ahead and, at a junction in the path, take the lower route. This leads to Missour, and shortly to Tissaldai (2,100m, 6-

*Azib Tifni*

7hrs. from Lac d'Ifni). There is a good campsite under walnut trees opposite the village.

## Day 6    *Tissaldai via Tizi-n'Terhaline to Azib Tamenzift*

Beyond the village the valley turns W and becomes narrower. Follow the track, which leads to an upland basin. Follow the stream then climb up a gully to the R of a knoll. The path to the L leads eventually to the same point, but is longer.

Emerge on top of the knoll. There is a small azib on the L, Irhir-n'Tarbaloute (2,630m). The track now starts to ascend the valley head, easily at first then directly up the hillside on the R via a series of zig-zags.

Gain the col, which is a smooth saddle on the ridge. This is the Tizi-n'Terhaline, (3,350m, called Tizi-n'Ounrar Imaghka on 1:100,000 maps). Ahead lies the upper Tifni basin, a high and remote area which leads into the upper Ourika valley.

The path which leads off to the L arrives eventually at the broad saddle of the Tizi-n'Tarharat. Don't take this, but drop straight down without undue difficulty into a valley which emerges at Azib

69

Tifni (2,820m), the small collection of huts below. This is another good example of a Berber azib; there isn't a building here over 1 metre in height.

From Azib Tifni there are 2 alternative routes:

a) Head back up the valley on the L for a short distance to the head of the cultivated section. From here head up the hillside in an easterly direction to reach the Tizi-n'Tifourhate (c.3,130m). Descend to Azib Amtou, the first village beyond the gorge (1hr.45mins. from Azib Tifni, 3hrs.45mins. from the col).

b) Follow the track through the gorge, crossing the river several times, to emerge below Azib Amtou. Longer, but less ascent and more interest. Continue along the L side of the valley to cross the Azib Tamenzift, the only village on the R bank. There is a good bivvy site next to the path by some large boulders 200 metres beyond the village. (Warning: kitbags have been stolen from here in the past.)

## Day 7    *Azib Tamenzift via Tizi Likemt to Tacheddirt*

From the bivvy site cross the river and follow the track diagonally up the hillside (E). This skirts the top of Azib Likemt, another summer residence where the highest building is no more than 3ft high (20mins.).

Continue N up the steep side valley on a good track, staying high to the L of the valley bed. The path leads (without shade) in 3hrs. to the col at the top, crossing scree for the last 400 metres.

The route arrives abrupty at the Tizi Likemt (3,555m). Look down the other side into the Imenane valley and be thankful that the pass is being ascended in this direction! Below lie some of the longest scree slopes you are likely to encounter in the region. The scree in the upper third is superb for running down (and horrible to ascend). Beyond this the scree becomes harder and less mobile. The route is painfully obvious, and leads straight down to the dirt road and a welcome spring.

If staying in the Tacheddirt CAF refuge head straight down from the road, passing terraces, to the river, ascend directly to Tacheddirt. Alternatively there is a good bivvy site reached by taking the dirt road R along the hillside. Pass boulders blocking the track, continue along until just before the road crosses the main river bed above

*Looking down the Upper Ourika valley*

Tacheddirt. The bivvy site is amongst large boulders just above a little gorge to the L.

From the col, it is possible to ascend Bou Iguenouane (3,882m, q.v.) via the WSW ridge (3hrs.30mins-4hrs. return to col).

*Day 8    Tacheddirt via Tizi-n'Tacheddirt to Ourika valley*
This day takes you into the remote upper Ourika valley which is rarely visited by trekkers.

From Tacheddirt follow the well-defined track up the valley to the Tizi-n'Tacheddirt (q.v., 3,230m, 2hrs.30mins.). At the col descend the well-defined track, following the L side of valley, to drop down zig-zags, arriving below rocky outcrops. Water hereabouts on R. Keep descending. After c.1hr.30mins. from the col a well-made path contours off to L - don't take this. The village of Labassene (c.2,240m) comes into view, high above the narrow valley floor. Take the higher path at the junction to enter above the village (2hrs.15mins. from the col, 4hrs.45mins. total).

Walk through the village to reach a well-made horizontal track, follow this to zig-zags down to the river (35mins. from village, 2hrs.50mins. from the col). The path contours above the river again. Suddenly the main Ourika valley comes dramatically into view: Timichchi is the village straight across on the opposite side of the valley, in the foreground is the small hamlet of Aguerd n'Ourtane. Take the higher path at the bifurcation just ahead, then drop straight down to Timichchi (1,850m, 4hrs.15mins. from the col, 6hrs.45mins. from Tacheddirt).

There is a village house in Timichchi belonging to the headman where food and accommodation are available. The refuge marked on 1:50,000 map is an old CAF hut, no longer in existence. For camping continue further up the valley to walnut groves. During the summer months it may be necessary to walk a km or so before running water is encountered.

Day 9 involves a long ascent; in summer parties may therefore wish to continue as far as Agounss, avoiding the worst of the heat with an early start.

## Day 9   Timichchi via Tizi-n'Ouhattar to Oukaimeden

As mentioned above this day involves a very long toil, over the Tizi-n'Ouhattar, another of the great Atlas passes and a masterpiece of route finding. Due to the relatively low altitude from which one commences, an early start pays dividends during the summer months.

From Timichchi cross the river bed to the L bank and follow the track (on the opposite side of valley to that shown on the 1:50,000 map) and the river bed. About 400m past Ait Chao, where the valley turns to the L, cross to the R banks and head steeply up what at first appears to be a dry gully bed. (25-30mins.). Emerge onto a track leading to Animiter. Impressive views of the N summit of Angour.

Continue through Tinoummer to Agounss, a large straggling village at the head of the valley (1hr.05mins.). Immediately on arrival, head back R up a zig-zag dirt track to enter the upper part of the village beneath the mosque. This is unmistakeable with its new concrete minaret. Pass beneath the mosque taking the L (horizontal) path (1hr.30mins.) which runs up through the village onto a stony path leading to the col, stay well to the R of the·large

*Beginning the long ascent of the Tizi n'Ouhattar,*
*Upper Ourika valley in the background*

solitary tree. This is a long hot slog without any shade, water or vegetation.

An abrupt finish brings one to the col, (3,140m, 4hrs.30mins.) and a dramatic contrast in scenery: ahead lies the grassy basin of Oukaimeden with its modern apartment blocks and radio mast.

There is a long descent to Azib Tiferguine (50mins. from the col) with a spring just before the azib. Continue down the valley and L across the grassy plain to Oukaimeden (2hrs. from col, 6hrs.30mins. total). Pass the CAF refuge before Chez Ju-Ju.

### Day 10   Oukaimeden - Gliz - Amsakrou

This and the next day's walk can easily be combined. However, by splitting the walk like this you have the opportunity to spend a night in Amsakrou, an interesting experience. It also means getting back to Marrakech at a reasonable time on the following day. (N.B. Amsakrou is written as Amskere on 1:50,000 maps.)

From Chez Ju-Ju follow the road up to the col (Tizi-n'Oukaimeden 2,682m) passing modern houses (15mins.). Drop down the RH side of the col on a good track. Ahead in the near distance is an obvious wooded, red earth ridge with a new dirt road on the R. The village of Agadir is just visible to the L of the ridge, over the saddle. Aim for Agadir, following the path until you are on a broad ridge with many junipers.

Reach a little knoll on the ridge where a path heads off L, take it down to fields and towards the villages of Agadir and Imsourene. About 300 yards before the first village, (1hr.) the path divides; carry straight on towards Imsourene and Agadir. Take the L fork which leads down the hillside. The path you take after the valley bottom is obvious, heading steeply up to a large grassy platform, then R to the col.

Follow the path down, crossing a new dirt road (which leads to a copper mine) to reach the attractive village of Gliz (1hr.20mins.). The narrow, steep main street provides plenty of good photo opportunities. It leads down out of the village to the river. Cross the river and ascend steeply (past a small waterfall) for 20mins. to reach the grassy platform at the RH end (1hr.55mins.).

A further 20mins. easy walking along a mainly level path leads

*Main Street, Gliz*

to the col (*c*.2,210m, 2hrs.15mins.). Good views ahead of the Tizi-n'Aguersioual, tomorrow's route. Take a good path down, contouring on the L hillside, and emerge above Amsakrou (50mins. from col, 3hrs.05mins. total).

Amsakrou is beautifully situated in a bowl surrounded by a fine series of terraces. Either stop in one of the village houses or camp by the river. As you enter the village from the RH side, the first house on the R in the horizontal street ahead takes in trekkers. Step inside this house and you are back in the Middle Ages. Notice the door-lock; it is made entirely of wood, even down to the wooden key. Narrow passageways lead out onto the flat roof of the house below.

### Day 11    *Amsakrou via Tizi-n'Aguersioual to Imlil*

Take the path-cum-drainage channel down the RH side of the village and wind your way down through terraces to the river. I invariably get lost here as the multitude of tracks is very confusing. If in doubt just keep heading downhill.

On the opposite bank is a series of newly-planted terraces of trees. Aim for the RH side of these, passing a few houses on the way. Once here the path is obvious. Follow it in 45mins. to the col, (Tizi-n'Aguersioual, *c*.2,030m) and a junction with the main Ikkis track which comes in from the L.

Take the track heading straight down to Aguersioual (1hr.40mins.). Walk through the village, which seems relatively affluent after Amsakrou, and at the wide, horizontal track, turn L. This leads pleasantly along the valley, soon dropping down to the river. Cross the river to regain the main road which leads in 45mins. to Imlil (2hrs.40mins.).

## Variations

Numerous variations are possible on this route, depending on time available.

### *From the Lepiney Refuge*

An easier alternative to the Tizi Melloul route is via the Tadat col. A good deal shorter, it nevertheless involves a fair amount of loose, unpleasant scree on the descent. This route is marked (blue dotted line) on the 1:50,000 map, and passes by the famous Tadat pinnacle (q.v.) on the col.

Take the path behind the refuge for a short way up the valley. Up to the L there is a large amount of scree beneath the cliffs. To the R a deep gully descends, not clearly seen from the refuge. When this becomes more apparent aim for the buttress on its L, just above the gully exit. Climb diagonally up the scree (loose, no real path), to gain the rocky ledges on the buttress, well above its toe.

Traverse R easily until the route above becomes clear: it follows the rocky rib just to the L of the gully bed and is cairned in places. Ascend for 100 feet or so to reach a narrow, grassy ledge with a large quartz-faced boulder on it. Take this ledge to its end, continue scrambling upwards (no technical difficulty) to where the gully widens into a steep cwm. Aim straight for the headwall above. Here there is a well-defined horizontal path which leads to an obvious gap in the ridge (2hrs.15mins.). The Tadat col can be clearly seen from here (across the other side of the bowl and slightly higher). Follow the horizontal track, crossing a snow patch half-way. Take care here - this was the scene of a fatal accident a few years ago. Climb the final short gully to arrive at Tadat col just below the pinnacle (c.3,720m, 2hrs.45mins.). At the col the view is dominated by Toubkal, directly across the valley. The S cwm route is clearly seen in its entirety. The Neltner refuge is not, however, visible.

Descend straight down the gully on steep scree, which gives a good run until it peters out. From here trend L to avoid the craggy section below. Soon, improbably, an ancient mule track is encountered. This track dates back to Roman times when copper and silver were mined here. Green veins of malachite can be seen everywhere around here. Take this track which leads down to arrive at a horizontal traverse below a low crag. Take this L as far as a spur.

The quickest way down from here is to aim for the bed of the main gully below. As you can see it is not a very attractive prospect. The alternative is longer but involves less actual scrambling.

Continue L along the traverse path until an obvious scree gully descends to the valley floor. Cross the head of the gully diagonally to the far side. Descend on L side of the gully to narrows, avoiding

*Kasbah Assaka - n'Ait Ouzzine*

the step, to gain easier grassy ground. Continue in this line until a faint diagonal track leads off R up the valley. Take this to the Neltner refuge (3,207m, 2hrs.30mins. from col).

## From the Neltner Refuge
It is possible to reach Azib Tamenzift in a day, rather than 3 days as per route above. This means going via the Tizi-n'Tarharat and omitting Lac d'Ifni. This is, however, a long walk.

From the Neltner refuge descend the valley to Sidi Chamarouch (1hr.15mins.). Cross the ford below the village (not the footbridge) and head back upstream to gain the path, which climbs quickly up the valley behind the Sidi Chamarouch shrine. Follow the zig-zags, passing after c.45mins. a track coming in from the R. (This is a shortcut from the Neltner refuge. Shortly before Sidi Chamarouch an obvious horizontal track crosses the hillside and emerges to join the main path.) Continue along the track, which zig-zags endlessly, to emerge eventually onto the bleak saddle at the summit of the Tizi-n'Tarharat (3,456m, 4hrs.45mins.), passing a spring after c.3hrs.30mins.

Take the well-defined path which leads off NE to contour across the hillside. This starts to trend E and leads to a steep spur. Descend this, which takes you to the head of the Azib Tifni pastures and rejoin the normal route at Azib Tifni (1hr.30mins. from the col).

## From Amsouzart
Rather than continuing up the Tissaldai valley it is possible to head directly to Azib Likemt via the Tizi-n'Ourai. As this would be a very long day from Lac d'Ifni, it is best to spend the night in Amsouzart.

Continue up the valley N as far as the next village on the R bank (Timzakine). Scramble up the hillside for a short way above the village to reach a good horizontal track. Follow this S., soon turning E to skirt a spur, then regaining the crest of this spur. Follow the track to a junction, take the L fork, leaving the spur. Continue in this line to gain the obvious col (Tizi-n'Ourai, 3,120m. This is called Tizi-n'Ououraine on 1:50,000 maps).

*Muleteers around campfire*

Descend on the track which parallels the stream. After *c.*500 metres take the higher path; don't drop down just yet. The main track leads to a confluence of two streams, cross here and follow the R bank of the stream down to emerge at a bivvy site just beyond Azib Tamenzift (7-8hrs.).

*From Tacheddirt*
It is possible to walk to Oukaimeden in a short day via the Tizi-n'Ouadi (2,928m).

Above Tacheddirt a broad track contours the hillside. Gain it and follow it to where it ends. Take the continuation track which leads towards a rocky rib. Where the track divides take the lowest path which soon starts to climb steeply. It leads to a false col, and the true col is 400 metres further on (1hr.45mins.).

Descent - take the very obvious track which leads down to the valley and the start of a motor road. Go past the ski-station to arrive in Oukaimeden by Chez Ju-Ju (3hrs.30mins.).

## Outlying Summits

These peaks are too far from the main bases to facilitate an easy ascent: they are included as being worthwhile objectives if time permits.

## Adrar-n-Dern (3,853m)

A large, featureless mound overlooking Amsouzart and the upper Souss valley. In reality of little interest, but useful as a link with Iferouane.

From Amsouzart head up the Tizgui valley towards Tissaldai. After a few hundred metres a track can be seen on the far spur of the deep valley to the R. Gain this track and follow it to the Tizi-n'Ourai (q.v. 3,109m).

Follow the ridge on the R which leads to the W spur (3,528m) Continue without difficulty to the main summit (3,853m). Immediately to the N there is a deep cwm separating Adrar-n-Dern from Iferouane.

## Iferouane (3,996m)

Marked as 4,001m on the 1:50,000 map, this probably accounts for the majority of ascents. It has, unfortunately, been revised down. A pleasant, if long, ridge walk from Adrar-n-Dern.

From Adrar-n-Dern skirt round the cwm to the N to reach a forepeak. Along the main ridge to gain the summit.

## Adrar Meltsen (3,595m)

A distinctive bulk which dominates the view down the upper Ourika valley. It can be climbed in a long day from Setti Fadma via the SW ridge (9hrs. from Setti Fadma). From the summit it is possible to follow a long crest NE to the hamlet of Ikis in the upper Zat valley. The road head is another day's walk down the valley from here.

## Taskka-n-Zat (3,912m)

The highest point on the south-bounding ridge of the Toubkal Atlas, difficult of access. Lying at the head of the Zat valley it can be reached from here in 2 days walking.

Hamish Brown has done a traverse of this ridge from the Tizi-n'Terhaline via Adrar-n-Dern to Taskka-n-Zat. A fine expedition taking several days (see bibliography).

## Yagour Plateau

A very large plateau to the NW of Setti Fadma, its principal attraction being the excellent prehistoric rock-carvings to be found on its flanks to the N of Azib Amdouz.

## Introduction

Although much less frequented by the visitor than the Toubkal region, the Mgoun massif is in fact within relatively easy reach of Marrakech and offers some of the most superlative walking anywhere in Morocco, as well as fabulous local architecture. A visit is well worth the effort.

The Mgoun massif, unlike the Toubkal region, consists of the typical sedimentary rocks of the High Atlas with their characteristic escarpments, long crested ridges (e.g. Tacheddid) and deep gorges, cut by the rivers through the softer rocks as the young fold mountains have risen. The summit of the Mgoun massif, variously called Irhil Mgoun or Amsod (4,068m) is the highest point in the Atlas outside the Toubkal area.

Described here is a 9-10 day circuit, which could quite feasibly be accomplished in a two-week holiday from Britain. Numerous variations are possible, and several of the days could be combined if time is short. One of the variations is a trip through the Tessaout gorge; this involves a small amount of climbing (up to V diff. in standard) for which a rope and slings are needed.

## Provisions

The Mgoun area differs from Toubkal in that here one passes through remote, roadless country where the only foods available are the occasional eggs, bread and potatoes. In autumn fresh fruit can be found, but in general it is safe to say that one needs to carry the bulk of one's supplies whilst on trek. Where small shops exist on route they are mentioned in the route notes.

## Approaches

From the north-west the usual point of departure is either Marrakech or Beni Mellal. Take the bus or service taxi to the large village of Ait Mohamed. There are shops here where one can buy the usual range

*Campsite looking towards the Arouss gorge descending from Irhil Mgoun*

of soft drinks and canned goods, together with vegetables and fruit (undependable), pots, pans and unappetising meat.

From Ait Mohamed onward travel becomes more difficult. The asphalt surface gives way a few kilometres beyond the village to rough track. Stretches of this track are definitely not for those of a nervous disposition! There are one or two trucks which service the Ait Bougoumez valley, the starting point for most of the treks, which park at the bottom of the main road in Ait Mohamed. Enquire on arrival when the next truck is due to depart: in summer 3 or 4 trucks on average leave per day.

It is best to arrive in Ait Mohamed as early as possible to ensure catching one of the trucks. It is a bone-jarring 3hrs.30mins. journey (signposted 48km) into the Ait Bougoumez valley, 4hrs.30mins. to Iskattafene. The road leads over a pass (the Tizi-n'Tirghist, 2,629m) and beneath the whaleback ridge of Azurki (3,690m), before dropping down through relic cedar and thuya woods to the Ait Bougoumez valley at Ifrane.

81

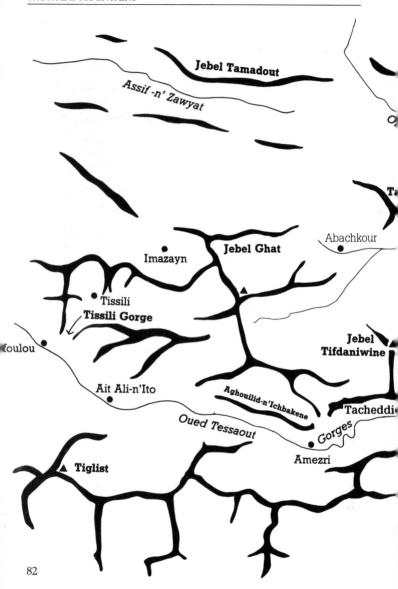

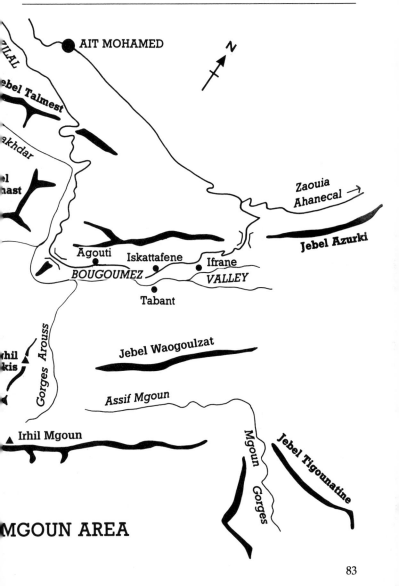

ILAL

ebel Talmest

akhdar

el
hast

AIT MOHAMED

N

Zaouia
Ahanecal →

Jebel Azurki

Agouti    Iskattafene    Ifrane

*BOUGOUMEZ*    *VALLEY*

Tabant

hil
kis

*Gorges Arouss*

Jebel Waogoulzat

Assif Mgoun

▲ Irhil Mgoun

*Mgoun Gorges*

*Jebel Tigounatine*

**MGOUN AREA**

Should you be unlucky and miss the trucks the alternatives are hitch-hiking or a taxi. There is an occasional passing pick-up truck, Land-Rover, or French trekking group Land-Rover. How likely the latter is to give a lift depends entirely on how full it already is. Hiring a taxi, needless to say, will be expensive, but should be obtainable for less than £30 from Ait Mohamed. Set against the cost of the holiday, it is certainly worthwhile.

## Valley Bases (Mule Hire and Local Guides)

Driving along the broad, flat Ait Bougoumez valley, one cannot help but be struck by the weird villages that line the road. The multi-storey mud-brick kasbahs make an interesting place to stay.

For the circuit described the starting point is the village of Iskattafene, towards the western end of the main valley. Here one can ask for accommodation in the village, and be directed to a suitable house. It is also a good place to hire mules. Alternatively, slightly up the valley is the larger village of Akchoui, again a good place to hire mules.

Elsewhere in the valley there are several houses used as a base by French trekking companies. There are also a few Moroccan guides who own houses in the valley:

Mohammed Achahri
Guide et Accompagnateur,
Ait Bougoumez,
P. Azilal.

Brahim Jellau,
Ait Bougoumez,
TAKHIDA P. Azilal.

Even if (as is likely) you do not desire a full guide service, they will offer assistance in obtaining mules etc. If you fancy local singing and drumming whilst on trek let Brahim or Mohammed know: the muleteers in their employ are usually also superb entertainers. Take advantage of this opportunity; it will result in a memorable trek.

*The local truck at the summit of the pass before descending to the Bougoumez valley*

Atlas Sahara Treks, run by Bernard Fabry, operate several treks both here and throughout the Atlas. The company maintains an attractive hotel, built in vernacular style, in Ifrane:

Atlas Sahara Treks,
72 Rue de la Liberté,
Marrakech. Tel: (4) 33757.

## A Circuit of the Region
*Day 1    Iskattafene - Abachkour*
From Iskattafene continue west along the dirt road, through villages, as after an hour or so it starts to climb gently to skirt the RH valley side. This valley is a delightful introduction to the area, with lush fields and walnut trees. Brilliantly-coloured rollers are the most common bird here.

Continue until a fine view is obtained of the deep valley ahead. Where the road splits take the LH branch beneath imposing rock walls. Descend to the village of Aguersif, passing a welcome fast-flowing stream (3hrs.30mins.).

Continue upstream (SW) to the large village of Iguelouene, where a couple of shops sell eggs, oil, sardines etc.

Turn L at the top of the village, to the R side of a large kasbah with a collapsed corner, continue on a mule track on the RH side of the valley. A strung-out collection of houses forms Abachkour (1,800m, 6hrs.30mins.). There is a good campsite by the river at the upper end of the village, beneath walnut trees.

*Day 2    Abachkour - Tarbat-n-Tirsal*
Head up the valley, passing the village of Ighboula on the R and a light-coloured kasbah up on the L. Walk firstly along a dry river bed (mid-summer onwards) then on a good mule track (steep at first) up to a col - the Tizi-n-Tighist (2,399m, 3hrs.). There are some very good prehistoric rock-carvings on sandstone rocks just to the NW of here, only a few yards from the track.

Continue on the track (well-defined) past a spring, on the S side of the valley, opposite the village of Tagassalt. Turn L along the broad, cultivated side valley before the main valley enters a rocky defile. Camp opposite the village (6hrs.).

*Day 3    Tarbat-n-Tirsal - Imazayn*

Follow a mule track in the SW valley below the cliffs of Jebel Ghat (also known as Jb. Rat, Rhat). Here you may well encounter black kites. Walk up to a col, skirting a subsidiary spur which runs down from the summit crest. Going around this spur the track fades. Keep on a slightly rising traverse until a further col is reached. Impressive views from here.

Drop down into the valley, heading WSW (steep in places) passing a good possible campsite. Where the path heads L to a saddle, take it L down to Imazayn, and then Tazaght just below (7hrs.). In Imazayn is a shop selling Coke, eggs, and few tinned goods and biscuits. Either stop in the village or cross the valley to camp on an obvious large, flat platform opposite the villages. (Water by a stone building just up behind the platform on the LH side.)

## Jebel Ghat

If time permits, this is a most worthwhile undertaking. The ridge as a whole would be a very long walk, probably taking 2 days.

From the campsite mentioned above (on descent to Imazayn), reverse the route to the col. The wearying ascent leads straight up from here to Pt.3564. Head WSW to the summit (5-7hrs.) A scree descent from here leads in 3hrs. back to the campsite. The route as a whole provides good, non-technical scrambling.

*Day 4    Imazayn / Tazaght via Tissili Gorge to Ifoulou*

From the large grass platform take the path on the RH side. This leads up over shaly ground into a stream bed (10mins.). Follow this small valley upwards and 30 yards after crossing a stream take the R bank and continue along a track parallel to the stream bed. (Spring over to the L after 35mins.)

Quit the stream bottom after 0.25 mile for the grassy ridge on the R. Follow the ridge path, mainly on the L side, to an obvious grassy col (1hr., *c*.2,550m). Descend in a southerly direction to an obvious track which follows a rocky spur straight down to a small azib. (Avoid the well-defined track contouring the hillside to the L - it

*The descent from Imi-n'Tizgui*

leads up into a high valley.)

From the lowest part of the azib:

1)	Follow the bed of the gorge, impressive and easy walking (but only if river is not in spate).

2)	Cross the river just below the azib, and take a mule track on the L side of the gorge. Again fine views, and route-finding is easy; just follow the path which obviously leads towards the end of the gorge.

Both routes arrive at the village of Imi-n-Tizgui. For the last 100 yards or so into the village, follow an irrigation channel on the RH side of the valley.

From Imi-n-Tizgui continue down the valley (much broader now) to Tissili (c. 1,980m, 3hrs.30mins.). This is a large, fairly affluent village with dirt road connections to the Haouz plain. There is at least one shop here which sells bread, eggs, and the usual selection of tinned sardines, biscuits etc. The Tissili gorge can be seen clearly from this village.

Descend to the river and follow the obvious gorge in the Serly direction. (Spring 0.25 mile after Tissili.) This is delightful, easy walking amidst impressive scenery. (In times of spate great care

*The valley at Imi-n'Tizgui*

needs to be taken with river crossings here.) Eventually you enter
the main Oued Tessaout valley (6.hrs.30mins.) between the villages
of Ifoulou (downstream) and Fakhour.

Campsite - 0.50 mile downstream towards Ifoulou there is a
pleasant level area of grass on the L bank. Mosquitos are a problem
here, as they are throughout the Tessaout valley.

*Day 5    Ifoulou - Fakhour - Ait Ali-n-Ito*
A very short walk, a relief after the last two tiring days. The route
follows the river the whole way.

Continue up the valley past Fakhour and Megdez to the next
large village - Ait Ali-n-Ito (2hrs.45mins.). Here there is an
unexpected gîte where one can stay cheaply. As you arrive the gîte
is the small building facing you at the furthest side of the village -
hollyhocks grow outside it. Inside, the house is elaborately decorated,
clearly a cut above its neighbours. Why it should be so, in such a
remote place, is hard to conceive. In any event the hot showers and
Hammam are most welcome. The guardian will also do a good tajine
or cous-cous, and has sackfuls of walnuts to eat with the mint tea.

89

**Variation**

For those who desire a more active day, proceed as follows: from Ifoulou a deep valley joins the main Oued Tessaout valley a few hundred yards downstream, on the S side. Follow this until a further valley comes in from the L. Take the track along this, which leads over a col. From the col descend into a valley, passing delightful waterfalls. Follow this valley, which leads past a large village to emerge at the main Tessaout valley, marginally upstream from Ait Ali-n-Ito.

*Day 6   Ait Ali-n-Ito - Ichbakene - Amezri*

The route follows the river the whole way. Once again crossings are made more difficult by heavy rain, and the route can be impassable in spring. Follow the main path, initially on the L side of the valley, passing a village with an interesting watermill just by the path. In 3hrs.30mins. reach Ichbakene. (N.B. Map wrong here! Ichbakene is wrongly positioned. In fact Ichbakene is approx. half-way between Amezri and Ait Ali-n-Ito.)

After Ichbakene cross the river to the R bank, the gorge becomes narrow and high-sided. Throughout this stretch of the river you pass fabulous, fairy-tale villages which owe nothing to the 20th century. The stark, rocky terrain and the absence of any roads adds to the feeling of other-worldliness. Unlike in the Ait Bougoumez valley, much of the building here is in stone. 1hr. beyond Ichbakene the valley opens out again at an azib, with a side valley coming in from the R. Keep following the river on the R bank and shortly enter an area of willows, take the path on the L bank.

Ahead the valley broadens considerably to form a large, cultivated basin. There is a prominent isolated kasbah on the R. Now one has the first decent view of the Mgoun massif - hitherto this has remained hidden. Continuing on the L bank of the Tessaout arrive shortly in the first village, Amezri (2hrs. from Ichbakene, 5hrs.30mins. from Ait Ali-n-Ito). Campsite - there is a pleasant campsite on a terrace beneath walnut trees, by the main path just before the village. Alternatively accommodation in the village should be easy to find.

*Day 7    Amezri - Source of Tessaout*

This is the day for which you have carried the rope and climbing equipment! Fortunately, as mentioned in the introduction, there is an alternative which goes via a col and doesn't involve any climbing.

If you have the ability to climb a 60 feet V diff. pitch, with sack if backpacking, then I cannot recommend the Tessaout gorge enough. The rock scenery is some of the most magnificent to be found anywhere, equalling if not surpassing anything in Europe. A canyon with 2,000ft walls, capped in places with huge jutting roofs, and crystal-clear waterfalls combine to make this a tremendous expedition.

Whichever route you decide to take, both initially continue up the Tessaout valley. From Amezri follow a track through the village along the irrigation channel, then head up L to a further settlement (40mins.). Keep contouring through fields until the river is reached, follow the R bank (1hr.05mins.).

Wade the river at a narrowing between rock walls, just past the concreted start of the irrigation channel. Continue on a track on the L bank to reach a well-defined horizontal track by a large cedar. This is where the 2 routes divide: for ascending the gorge continue upstream. If taking the easier (though longer) way, turn L along the horizontal track.


*Via Tessaout Gorge*

Continue up the path to where a path joins the river at a small bridge - the Tessaout-n'Oufla. Keep on the L bank. The path taken in times of flood, described above, is the one crossing the bridge. It follows the easier route via the col to the campsite.

The river bends L and becomes narrow again. The path crosses a crag 50 feet above the river - straightforward but narrow and airy for a short distance. Continue up the gorge, taking the easiest line on either bank, passing the occasional deserted shelter built into the caves. These are reminiscent of American Indian *pueblos* such as the Canyon de Chelly. These and the hewn cedar logs provide evidence that the Berbers have been here before. Even more remarkable are the little bridges and wooden stairs built across awkward sections. Locals assure me that they take donkeys up

*The campsite above the Tessaout gorge, with a natural rock arch in the middle distance, Mgoun lies to the right*

here, though the path is too difficult for mules.

The gorge continues, winding its way in a bewildering series of twists and turns, becoming ever more enclosed and towering. The vegetation here is lush alongside the river, reflecting the absence of the ubiquitous goats. After approx. 4hrs. a 'bad step' of 35 feet is encountered by a waterfall. This is climbed just L of the waterfall. Moderate in standard.

Continue past a remarkable little spring emerging from the rock wall, to reach an impassable waterfall 30mins. further on. Circumventing this is the crux of the whole ascent. From the broad rock platform by the river, (just below and out of sight of the waterfall), there is an obvious crack on the R wall of the gorge. It starts from ledges some 30 feet above the scree and leads to a terrace. Scramble up to the base of the crack and climb it (V diff., 65 feet, at least 2 good pegs in place) to the terrace. Be careful of loose rock on the floor of the terrace. Belay well back.

From here easy scrambling and walking leads past some huge

*Above: The Taggourt Plateau*

*Below: Part of the Dades Gorge*

boulder chokes. The gorge starts to lose height rapidly. Continue along it to emerge eventually onto a beautiful upland pasture and campsite. There is a natural rock arch 100 yards ahead on the right.

## Via the Col

From the junction in the gorge take the horizontal track L and follow a good path NW past an azib (where there is a faint trickle of water only in summer). Begin to bear R, zig-zag up to a prominent gully beneath a series of buttresses. Follow the path almost to the top of the gully, bear R with it to a col. (c.3,216m). This is the highest point reached. At the col a faint path bears L across the Tacheddid plateau. (Poor quality water 1hr. beyond the col.) Wander in and out of a broken crag system for a further 1hr.30mins. Bear R downhill on a good path towards the top of the gorge. The meadow campsite is visible ahead.

## N.B. If the River is in Spate

From Amezri take the track which leads across the head of the main valley floor towards the RH branch of the upper valley. A good mule track leads around the hill between the two branches, and skirts L to arrive back in the main gorge at the small bridge mentioned. Cross this, and proceed as for the route via the col.

## Day 8    The Ascent of Mgoun

The highest point in this part of the Atlas, and the only 4,000m peak outside the Toubkal region. The actual summit is Amsod (4,068m) which is only one part of a long ridge, however, that stretches for several miles at around 4,000m. The ascent is straightforward with no technical difficulty.

From the campsite follow the main valley NE to where it opens into a wide plain (20mins.). Trend R towards a distant summit on the flat side valley. Aim towards a 'block-house' shaped solitary rock straight ahead on the crest of a nearby hill (E). Follow this into the valley, to the base of a spur descending from the main ridge. Skirt the base of the mountain (ENE) to the valley. Zig-zag up (50mins.), continue to a large spur, cross this into a gully and find a prominent track. Continue in the same direction towards a very obvious col and well-defined track - the Tizi-n-Oumsoud (3hrs.).

At the col skirt L on the S side and head up the scree (tiring) to reach the main ridge. Follow this to Pt.3967 (4hrs.30mins.), rocky top. There are permanent snow patches here and frost striations, an indication of conditions in winter. Sacks can be left here as you return this way. It is still a long way to the summit, though. Continue along a delightful ridge, superb views if no haze, to Pt.4011 (5hrs.15mins.) and on to the summit (4,068m, 6hrs. from camp).

Descent: return along the ridge to Pt.3967 (1hr.15mins. from the summit), then down the scree, facing back towards the main summit initially, skirting L under Pt.3967 to drop to a rocky depression which leads into a deep, broad, stony valley. Descend steeply into this valley which runs NNW to the main one, and head back to the campsite (2hrs.30mins from Pt.3967, 9hrs.30mins-10hrs. for the whole trip).

## Day 9   Via Tacheddid Ridge to Iskattafene

The final day's walking offers excellent views, and the first suitable opportunity to see the general course of the previous week's walking.

From the campsite follow the main valley for 150 yards before it drops away. Head L towards the Tacheddid ridge. Ascend a zig-zag path which trends towards the end of the ridge. Reach the crest (2hrs.10mins.) with a good viewpoint 100 yards to the R along the ridge. From the crest follow an obvious track, first NW towards Jebel Tifdaniwine, the prominent pyramidal peak, then down to an azib and R down a steep valley, passing a welcome spring half-way down.

(Jebel Tifdaniwine (3,449m) is an obvious possibility, if feeling fit, from the Tacheddid ridge. Traverse the hillside to the L to gain the ridge at the saddle connecting Tifdaniwine to the main Tacheddid ridge. Follow this directly to the summit. Descent: either retrace your steps to the main ridge, or drop down from the saddle directly to the azib.)

Continue down to a small hamlet (4hrs.) then to Arouss, then the village of Ait Said just before the main Ait Bougoumez valley. Head R into the valley across a stony plain to arrive at the dirt road just

*Looking towards the summit of Mgoun, with the
Tizi-n'Oumsoud the prominent col on the right*

*Looking towards Ighil n'Ikkis from the Tacheddid ridge,
Behind right  lies the Ait Bougoumez valley*

before Iskattafene (6-6hrs.30mins.).

## Variation

An interesting variation is possible, involving a short abseil. Where the upland plain starts to drop away (a few hundred metres after the track turns L to ascend the Tacheddid ridge), follow the gully down steeply to reach the stream bed. Follow the stream bed into the gorge.

The gorge is very narrow in places, where the river has cut through the severely folded rock. The waterfall is circumvented by a short abseil, using a stake on the L for belay. The abseil leads (literally) into the pool at the base of the waterfall. Follow the base of the gorge, still interesting but easy, to emerge in a broad, willow valley. This soon leads to a junction with the normal route.

If you desire to see the gorge without having to abseil turn R (upstream) at the first village. (Good campsite by the river.) Follow the river until it enters the gorge, which can in turn be followed as far as the waterfall. Immediately on entering the gorge from below, notice the slender cascade high on the L. This is very beautiful and easily missed when descending. It is possible to scramble easily up to the base of this fall, which is set back from the main gorge.

## Other Excursions in the Mgoun Area

The long ridges and escarpments provide ample scope for day and multi-day walks. Unlike the ridges in the Toubkal region these present few technical difficulties. The following list merely gives an indication of the potential; visitors will undoubtedly discover routes of their own.

## Mgoun (4,068m)

The continuation ridge NE from the summit provides a magnificent walk, which leads eventually into the Mgoun gorges.

Mgoun can be reached from the S, and this is perhaps, one of the easiest ways of ascending the peak. Own transport is essential, however. From Ouarzazate drive to Skoura, then north to Amekchoudand and on to the roadhead at Aguerd-n'Igherm. From here head NE straight up the valley to Tighouzzirine, from where

*Ascending screes to the summit ridge of Mgoun from the Tizi-n'Oumsoud*

a track leads northwards onto the spur desending from the summit ridge. Head steeply up to gain a subsidiary ridge, which leads to the main ridge and the summit.

### Tacheddid
Another fine ridge walk, this time with some scrambling involved. From the campsite beneath Mgoun it is a 6-8hr. round trip.

### Azurki (3,690m)
The very prominent limestone escarpment bordering the northern side of the Ait Bougoumez valley. From the col on the road into the valley it provides an enjoyable day's walk.

### Aioui (3,382m)
A continuation of the Azurki ridge eastwards. Its eastern flanks provide some excellent rock-climbing.

## The Mgoun Gorges

The Mgoun gorges to the E of the main Mgoun ridge are very impressive. They can be approached from the south by driving from El Kelâa des Mgouna  N to Issoumar. Alternatively, from the Ait Bougoumez valley, several tracks lead over Jebel Waogoulzat into the remote upper Mgoun valley above the gorges.

*Looking along summit ridge from pt. 3967m.*

## Introduction

South of the main Atlas range, the region is drained by the Dades and Draas valleys. In contrast to the greener, more fertile slopes to the north, the landscape here is one of vivid oases set beneath barren mountain slopes. Palm trees abound, and roses form hedgerows between small fields. The roses are an important crop, being used to produce attar.

Architecturally, the region is stunning, with countless mud-brick kasbahs lining the road. Unfortunately, as in other areas, these are falling into disrepair, but sufficient remain to provide a spectacular sight.

Noteworthy in this respect are Skoura, the huge Kasbah at Ouarzazate, and the lower Dades area. Even if there is no time for walking, it is worth spending a couple of days exploring this area.

The Jebel Sahro is a range of mountains between the High Atlas and the Sahara, the eastern continuation of the Anti-Atlas.

Starkly beautiful, it offers a sense of isolation not to be found in the more populated ranges. Barely visited by westerners, the inhabitants seem more hospitable and friendly as a result.

The Jebel Sahro is a region of contrasts. One minute a trail may lead beneath date palms or through almond groves watered by an ancient well, the next minute it may cross a stony plateau where nomads in their black felt tents scrape a living. The atmosphere is biblical, with shepherds playing reed flutes commonly heard. Camels are occasionally seen too, silhouetted against the skyline. The scenery is often magnificent with flat-topped mesas and buttes forming a backdrop to deep gorges and tottering pinnacles of conglomerate.

As a whole the area possesses a magic which will appeal to anyone with a sense of adventure. It is not without its problems and hazards: this is wild country, with neither road nor telephone, the people are unused to visitors and so dealings can take some time.

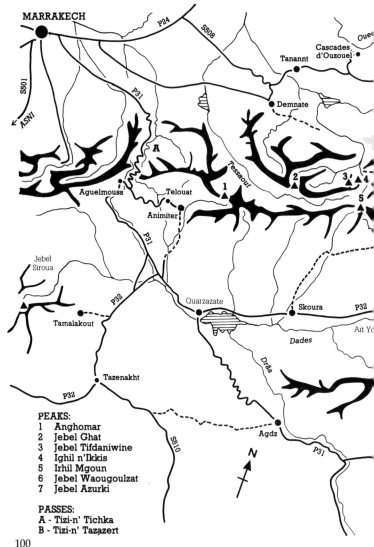

PEAKS:
1   Anghomar
2   Jebel Ghat
3   Jebel Tifdaniwine
4   Ighil n'Ikkis
5   Irhil Mgoun
6   Jebel Waougoulzat
7   Jebel Azurki

PASSES:
A - Tizi-n' Tichka
B - Tizi-n' Tazazert

**THE CENTRAL HIGH ATLAS
AND JEBEL SAHRO**

The best time to visit is from October through to March, outside these months it is likely to be uncomfortably hot. In the winter months, however, do not underestimate the cold. There is a heavy frost on most nights and during the day it can be bitterly cold as well. Snow is usual in January but normally during this period one can expect to find the sun shining and temperatures in the mid-60°s to 70°s. It is essential to bring a good 4-season sleeping bag, and preferably a duvet jacket for the long, cold nights.

The circuit described below is a 9-day tour (allowing for time spent purchasing supplies, hiring mules etc.) which could easily be done in a two-week holiday from Marrakech or Agadir.

## Approaches

Marrakech and Agadir both serve as suitable starting-points. From Marrakech go via the Tizi-n'Tichka to Ouarzazate, then E along the P32 to Kelâa des Mgouna (6hrs. driving time). From Agadir go inland as far as Ouarzazate, then join the route from Marrakech as described above.

Buses depart regularly from Marrakech and Agadir for Ouarzazate. Continuing E along the P32 there are plenty of local buses and shared taxis. There is an airport at Ouarzazate, from where there are flights to Europe, a Club Med. and various other large hotels.

One of the pleasant surprises a visitor to the South side of the Atlas finds is the number of good hotels. The area is very popular with the French in winter, and it is possible to sleep and dine in comparative luxury here.

## Town Supplies

There are several large towns along the Dades valley which makes the purchase of supplies relatively easy and means it is not really necessary to stock up in Marrakech.

Ouarzazate is the largest and best-stocked town, though furthest from the mountains. Western foods are best purchased here, otherwise continue on to Kelâa where everything needed can be obtained, and where there is a large market (reasonably priced). Furthermore Kelâa is much the closest town to the start of the trek.

Boumalne, 22km NE along the valley, is similar though smaller and with much less choice. Further E, Tinerhir is similar to Boumalne in variety of shops.

Ouarzazate, Kelâa and Boumalne have hospitals and chemists.

## Supplies en route

It would be hard to eat well here on food purchased en route. Bits and pieces are available, but don't rely on these when stocking up. It is best to regard them as variety, rather than as staples.

Eggs and dried dates can be found in most villages, and in more unlikely places too; sometimes a small girl will run over from her flock of sheep and hold out a handful of eggs. In the villages chickens are not expensive, and delicious bread can often be found. Elsewhere a sheep or goat can always be purchased, the muleteers will happily prepare it over an open fire. Occasionally almonds are available, but these are an important cash crop and are not sold cheaply.

Gas refills are not available anywhere so be sure to take sufficient with you. For lighting fires there is an abundance of dry brush, which flares up quickly. This isn't much use for cooking over, but it is what the locals use.

Finally, the cleanest supply of water is often in the wells. These may not have buckets attached so it is worth carrying some string for lowering water bottles.

## Bases
### Ait Youl

The circuit described starts and finishes in the village of Ait Youl, S of Kelâa des Mgouna, on the edge of the barren valley plain. From the main street turn R just after the market (when heading towards Boumalne), then head along a stony track for 4km to the N bank of the Dades river. Cross via a footbridge into the village. The local mosque and minaret is a prominent landmark on the southern fringes of the village.

It is possible to hire mules here, and local guides. The houses will take in visitors, for a small charge (try the house on the very edge of the village, approx. 250m SE of the minaret). If you arrive late in the evening spend the night in Kelâa, accommodation is hard to find

103

here after everyone has locked and bolted the entrance to their courtyard.

## Iknion

40km SE of Boumalne is the best base for exploring the eastern section of the Jebel Sahro, including Jebel Fengour and Amalou n'Mansour. Several trekking groups use Iknion as a base. It has the advantage of familiarising the locals with trekkers' needs, but it can be a disadvantage if a group is in the area as there will be fewer mules available for hire.

## Nkob

Often groups trek to Nkob on the SE flanks of the range. Smaller than Iknion it has fewer facilities, but mules can be hired here. Access to the main eastern part of the range is fairly easy from here.

## A Circuit of the Region

*Day 1    Ait Youl - El Mersse Puit*

This first day's walking is rather tedious as it involves crossing the wide, stony expanse between the Dades river and the mountains proper. However, as it is the first day on trek, boredom is alleviated somewhat by the novelty of everything.

From the new minaret in Ait Youl head SE towards an obvious low valley across the stony plain. Trend R to reach a small cultivated area on the banks of a wadi (20mins.) where there is a prominent long, low house above the trees. Pass the house on its R (S) side via a decent mule track, heading SSE, leaving the valley.

Some 300 metres beyond the house enter a tiny, dry valley, follow the L bank for another 200-300 metres or so and emerge onto a low plateau spur. The path continues across this spur to descend into a larger valley. Cross this diagonally (45mins.) and keep heading S. The near hill to the SE is Afoughal (2,196m). Its eastern flanks are skirted on the return route.

Continue roughly S, skirting a basin on the L. Cross a little ridge (1hr.) to enter another broad valley. Follow the track on the L. After 10mins. of this the path turns R (still going S) and crosses the valley floor. A further 5mins. leads to the main wadi bed (1hr.15mins.).

Walk along this (usually some water in winter), passing a concrete well and drinking trough whose water is filthy and stagnant (1hr.25mins.). A few hundred metres beyond the well the river bed bends to the L - keep straight on SE. Pass a small stone enclosure 50 metres further on on the L. Trend R to regain the Serly direction (1hr.35mins.) and join a motorable track.

All the previous section is vague and indistinct on the ground, route-finding becomes much easier as the day progresses.

After 2hrs. or so the path branches R off the main track, heading straight towards the distant highest peak on the southern skyline. It leads down into another big valley, with a prominent black rock island in its bed. There is a small settlement below this, the track leads to the L of the houses in *c.*2hrs.40mins. The good track continues along the valley, passing a fourth pisé house and courtyard; the low, square plan contrasts strongly with the previous house's rectangular ksar arrangement and tower in the centre N wall. Continue past a small house with a large tree which is very distinctive. There is a well here with good water but no bucket.

The path trends R (S) here and forsakes the main valley for a little valley on the R. Continue towards Afoughal and a house on its northern flank. Just before this is a stream and a tiny rocky gorge. Skirt the mountain on the R, heading S. In 4hrs.25mins. you reach a good, large well on the edge of fields (a fine lunch spot).

Continuing S enter a narrowing valley with a fair amount of thorn vegetation and running water. At a stone 'blockhouse' (5hrs.30mins.) the path keeps L (S) below the crags. Ahead is a large basin (before it a deep ravine), which is delightfully verdant. Cross the ravine, and a further 10mins. across the plain see trees on the R. These trees mark the site of the puit (well) at El Mersse. Good campsite (6hrs.30mins.).

## Day 2    *El Mersse Puit - Assaka-n'Ait Ouzzine*

From the well at El Mersse head NE across the plain to an obvious low point on the skyline. After 200 metres however, gain a track heading SE which leads diagonally across the hillside to a ridge top (35mins.). Here there are fantastic views of the Mgoun ridge and along the main Atlas chain as far as Toubkal. To the W Jebel Siroua

*Outlying pinnacle, Tassigdelt Tamajgalt.*
*The ascent route described takes the chimney between the two towers*

*Chamaux, L. and un-named tower overlooking the Taggourt plateau*

is prominent in isolation, and the Dades valley unfolds beneath you. Ahead, the landscape is craggier, with low scrub covering the hillsides. The prominent large plateau to the SE is Keftent (2,095m).

The well-defined track continues in a Serly direction to reach the Tizi-n'Tagmout (1,754m) in 1hr.30mins. Drop down into the broad valley, which possesses a few scattered houses and trees. The route now begins to head E towards the central Jebel Sahro. Take the path ENE along the broad valley, which is flanked by Amgroud (2,259m) to the S. Ahead lies a very prominent flat-topped mesa - Tine Ouaiyour (2,129m).

The valley bottom narrows as the path takes the S side above the wadi bed. Assaka-n'Ait Ouzzine comes suddenly into view, with its beautiful old kasbah, fruit and palm trees (4hrs.40mins.). Don't enter the village, but keep on the near bank of the wadi and head S to where it turns W. After a few hundred metres of following the wadi bed (5hrs.) turn back S up a low ridge to join another tributary (5hrs.05mins.). Walk along this tributary in an easterly direction for 5mins. to enter another, smaller village known as part of

Assaka-n'Ait Ouzzine, (5hrs.10mins.). From its eastern end one can see a very fertile area on the opposite bank with a ruined kasbah. The soft, water-soluble nature of the pisé walls means that such buildings have only a 20-30 year life once they are abandoned.

## Day 3    Assaka-n'Ait Ouzzine - Irhazzoun n'Imlas

Continue eastwards along the valley, wonderfully fertile in comparison with the previous two days. Note the well, complete with old wooden pulley wheel (10mins.). After 1hr. reach another small village, Tajalajt. There are signs of modernisation here, with diesel-engined water pumps and new houses.

Continue to the next village Akerkour (1hr.40mins.), a small hamlet with a few well-watered fields. The bulbuls here are very vocal in amongst the palms. Keep walking along this valley which suddenly opens out (3hrs.30mins.). The mountain ahead to the E is Tassigdelt Si el Haj (1,722m) which has some impressive escarpments.

After 4hrs.45mins. and heading in a roughly ENE direction, you encounter a few houses around a river meander with several fields. All along this stretch of valley the churring of sandgrouse can be heard; they are extremely secretive birds and difficult to spot.

Continuing NE the scenery becomes ever more arid and assumes an aspect reminiscent of the American south-west: broad scrub plains, flat-topped mesas and buttes. The path leads beneath a huge cliff on the R (the largest seen so far) to gain a small col. At the col (6hrs.) is the first view of the Bab-n'Ali, or Gates of Ali: this is the huge pinnacle in the distance looking E with the eroded pinnacles of the Tadaout n'Tablah to its L.

Head initialy E then drop down, after 200-300 metres, into a gully. The prow of the cliff is very impressive from this angle. Continue down to the broad plain and the village of Irhazzoun n'Imlas (6hrs.30mins.).

## Day 4    Irhazzoun n'Imlas via Taggourt Plateau to Igli

Head initially towards the Bab n'Ali pinnacle (E), then veer slightly L towards an isolated building. Growing on the borders of the fields here, seemingly abandoned, are tiny round melons. Don't bother

*Un-named tower, Taggourt plateau*

tasting them, they are extremely bitter.

Walk along the sandy wadi bed, which contains one or two palm trees and some very brackish water. This soon becomes a gorge and just as soon finishes (30mins.). Ahead lies a fine pinnacled rock formation: the Tadaout n'Tablah. Cross the slabs to gain a track above the wadi bed which leads NNE out of the wadi. Emerge (45mins.) onto the edge of another wadi, with further fantastic organ-pipe rock formations ahead. The path winds its way towards the nearest formations (super views looking back from here). Aim to the L (N) of this formation (the Tadaout n'Tablah) and gain a slight ridge. The view from here is even better with the Tête de Chamaux (Camel's head) and Tassigdelt Tamajgalt formations appearing for the first time, along with other equally fantastic plugs and spires.

You are now on the Taggourt plateau. Just to the L (2hrs.10mins.) is a cliff, over which the stream flows, and a couple of palm trees. On my first visit here I was welcomed by an old man with a plateful of dates. He was living in a black felt tent nearby with a wife who looked forty years younger than himself, and their three children.

As she was baking on an open fire I waited until the bread was ready and purchased a few loaves. This was life at its most basic; there was nothing superfluous amongst their few meagre possessions. The woman wore exquisite, heavy silver jewellery and brilliantly-patterned clothes, but otherwise there was no ornamentation to their existence.

The route continues across the plateau towards the Tête de Chamaux in a NNE direction. As this is a short day you may wish to explore the Tadaout n'Tablah pinnacles. To do so, instead of continuing across the plateau, head NE to gain the gap between the two LH rock masses. At the gap a gully leads easily up onto the top of the Tadaout n'Tablah plateau. On top there are fine views all around, with nearby towers and the twin plugs of the Bab n'Ali to the SE.

Back on the normal route the huge isolated plug on the L has cairns on top (climbed by whom is a mystery). Drop down from the edge of the plateau (the Tizi n'Taggourt, 2hrs.30mins.) into a valley which has one or two fields and a house on top of a ridge. The track weaves through fields, past further houses, heading towards the Tête de Chamaux again. At the end of the fields (3hrs.20mins.) head steeply up the R bank. This leads in 10-15mins. to a further cultivated area and one or two houses in a cirque, hemmed in by cliffs on three sides. This is Igli (3hrs.35mins.) a rest spot for the night. The Tête de Chamaux (see below) makes a good afternoon excursion from here.

## Day 5    Igli

It is worth spending a day in this area to explore the surrounding cliffs. Directly above the campsite to the NE is the Tassigdelt Tamajgalt, while to the NW is the long Tête de Chamaux. Of the two the Tassigdelt Tamajgalt is the more worthwhile, although both can be done in one day. ESE lies the nearby conical point of Isker (2,099m), not nearly as interesting as its neighbours.

Tassigdelt Tamajgalt is a large, cliff-ringed plateau. On its Sern edge there is an outlier separated by a rift several tens of metres wide. The top of this outlier can be gained from its eastern flanks by following a system of gullies. It is terrific fun exploring these clefts

*Igli*

in the rock: the route I took to the summit passed between the main cliff body and an outlying spire (70-100m) with an ancient pine decorating its summit. The gap is only 1-2 metres wide, and spanned by a chockstone. Further crawling under boulders and easy scrambling gains the top. No doubt future visitors will find alternative routes for themselves.

This massif, and all the other rock pinnacles in this area, are formed from a soft 'pudding-stone' conglomerate. On the summit of the outlier there is a thin capping band of hard, but soluble limestone, down through which the water has cut and eroded the softer 'pudding-stone' below. This has created the very deep fissures which criss-cross this entire outlier and are, for the most part, narrow enough to step or jump over. Some of the larger gullies contain sizeable ash trees. On top, the flat summit is covered in white alyssum. One can only wonder what the vegetation of this region would be like, without the ever-present sheep and goats.

On the western side of the block is a pinnacle reminiscent of the 'lost arrow spire', separated from the main outlier by a 5 metre gap. Unclimbed as yet, it offers interesting possibilities to climbers who

111

visit this area. Visible from the outlier summit (behind and just R of Isker) is Jebel bou Rhdad (2,334m). The low ridge to the R on the near skyline is a large, flat-topped plateau called Jebel Aneffid.

When you tire of exploring this wonderland move across to the Tête de Chamaux. This is easily reached by aiming for the lowest point of the tower on its LH (southern) edge. Unlike its neighbour, the top here cannot be reached by scrambling, and as far as I am aware has yet to be climbed. Several pairs of Barbary falcons nest here. It is possible to skirt the base of the cliffs right around the tower, with only a short (8 metre) section of easy scrambling at the northern end.

## Day 6    Igli - Tamourt

This is another very good day, with an optional ascent of a rocky peak by the Tizi-n'Ouarg. The route passes initially via the reddish rock intrusion between Tassigdelt Tamajgalt cliffs. The path leads above the gully bottom, up through rock slabs, and through ground rich with chewed palm fronds and bushes. It then moves well to the R, out of the gully bed, and traverses horizontally. Barbary ground squirrels are common here, providing good food for the hawks which nest amongst the crags.

Follow this path, which leads to the top in 1hr.40mins. and emerges onto a hummocky rock plateau I recall hearing a shepherd playing a reed pipe in the midst of this desolation. Drop down to a wadi which makes a 90° bend on arrival; the Tizi-n'Ouarg is straight ahead to NNE. (**N.B.** At this point the escape route to Tiouit heads E along the little tributary wadi on the R.) Cross the stream and ascend to the L (W) side. A gradual ascent leads into the bowl surrounded by tops known as Kouaouch (2hrs.55mins.). Looking back, the N side of Tassigdelt Tamajgalt is revealed as a gentle slope. If time and energy permit, it is worth climbing the little peak to the N: 8-10 metres of easy scrambling on the S face to gain the summit overlooking the precipitous N face (c.80 metres). There are outstanding views from here in all directions, from the snow-capped Mgoun ridge to the Tazzarine valley in the S.

Walk on to the Tizi-n'Ouarg (3hrs.20mins.) and descend S of W. A distinctive feature on the descent are the 20 or so trees which are scattered on the slope. Drop down between rounded tops and continue in a roughly WSW direction. In 45mins. from the col you reach a small, flat grassy area by a stream, below the peak of Tamourt. This is a good campsite, though cold due to the altitude (4hrs.05mins.).

## Day 7    *Tamourt - Irhissi*

Continue WSW across featureless pasture until the valley starts to pass beneath the large bulk of Jebel Amlal on its S side. The valley becomes flanked by tall cliffs. Follow the stream down as it leads beneath impressive crags. Half-way down the valley there are a few small shelters belonging to the semi-nomadic herders who scratch a living here. 10mins. beyond the houses there is another small shelter on the R. Just before this on the LH side are several graves. Graves in these parts are simple affairs, being a low pile of stones with a solitary, uninscribed headstone. Once recognised, many similar burial areas close to paths and habitation become apparent.

At the bottom of this valley to the SW you reach a small settlement - Foudoud. The track winds behind it then climbs steeply up and over the ridge. Descend from the ridge into a small valley and follow it down, through increasingly impressive scenery, to arrive at a ruined kasbah at the confluence of two valleys. This is Irhissi (6hrs.30mins.) and makes a fine camping place.

## Day 8    *Irhissi via Assaka n'Ait Ouzzine to Tafoughalt*

This is another fairly long day with a steep ascent after lunch. Rather than continuing in a SW direction, it is more interesting to skirt the flat-topped bulk of Tine Ouaiyour (2,129m) via its southern side.

From the field near the kasbah, cross the stream to its Sern bank and enter the narrow gorge, (Gorge du Irhissi), which heads S almost immediately. Follow the zig-zag track pleasantly up through the gorge to emerge after 25mins. opposite small conglomerate cliffs. Tine Ouaiyour is very close now. Gain the top of the gentle spur after 50mins. There is another simple graveyard by the track here. Fine view E towards Tassigdelt Tamajgalt, and on the R skyline in the far distance, Jebel Bou Gaffer. The near mountain N of E is Jebel Amlal.

The track leads round Tine Ouaiyour to the SW flank. After 1hr.20mins. you skirt a gully - don't take the path on its L (opposite) bank. 6-7mins. further on your path starts to descend gently SW to the valley. Cross the undulating plain, and after *c.*2hrs.40mins. see on the L the deep valley taken on the morning of day 3. The path keeps high on the L bank. After 4hrs.05mins. Assaka-n'Ait Ouzzine comes into view - one is better able to appreciate the architecture from this viewpoint than from the other side of the valley.

Continue through Assaka-n'Ait Ouzzine passing between a kasbah on the L and a ksar on the R (noticing the difference in styles). Head R up through the village and continue N across rock slabs to gain a faint path. Cross the ridge (4hrs.20mins.) and descend to a solitary palm tree. The route then winds up the hillside towards big crags and no apparent exit.

Pass the RH toe of a large crag (5hrs.30mins.), continue up the gully and finally emerge on easier-angled ground (5hrs.45mins.). The summit of Tine Ouaiyour is now well below you, but the top of the pass is still another 35mins. away. This affords stunning views both N and S. To the N the Mgoun ridge is prominent, L of this is Annrhomar and to the R the prominent split in the range marks the Gorge du Dades. Further W Meltsene and the Toubkal massif are visible, while below stretches the Dades valley.

Descend E paralleling the ridge, walk along a spur NE (5mins. from the top, 6hrs.25mins.). Drop down to the L, this leads in the general direction of Afoughal to the NNW, down to a solitary house and fields in a flat basin surrounded by low granitic-looking rock outcrops. This is Tafoughalt (7hrs.35mins.).

*Day 9    Tafoughalt - Ait Youl*
100 metres W of the house head R (N) across a low rocky rise, past a prominent large, upright boulder. W of N is a gap on the skyline through low bouldery ridges. The path weaves its way here (10mins.). A sudden view of the Dades valley makes you realise the height of the previous night's campsite.

Drop down the valley, passing Afoughal on the L. After 1hr.05mins. pass houses by the path on the L above. 5mins. further on there is a gully, either side of which are caves inhabited seasonally by nomads. It is common to see nomads on this route as an agreement exists between those of the Ait Bougoumez region, and those of the Jebel Sahro. In summer the nomads of the Jebel Sahro ascend to the central High Atlas, whose nomads in turn make a winter migration down to here.

Cross a spur on the W bank of the main wadi (1hr.15mins.) and continue in the same direction. After 2hrs.20mins. pass more caves on the R, this time for goats. The trail starts to leave the main valley bed for its E side, heading first NNW, then N up a tributary. Head steeply up past some more caves for several hundred metres and, with diversions NW, gain a col after 2hrs.55mins.. Follow the track down to where it joins a motor track after 4hrs.10mins.. Leave the motor track almost immediately, keeping on down the valley, until, after 15-20mins., the path ascends the hill ahead.

At the top you can see down into the Dades valley, but can't see Ait Youl as yet. After 4hrs.40mins. you emerge onto a ridge which is followed round and leads eventually to the prominent white minaret of Ait Youl and the end of the circuit.

## Continuation: Valley Walk to Boumalne

If time permits, it is possible to walk along the Dades valley from Ait Youl to Boumalne. A contrast to the previous days on trek with walking through fields and orchards. One realises why this is known as the Valley of the Roses; every field and irrigation ditch is lined with low rose bushes. In total the walk is around 14 mile (22km) but can easily be terminated simply by heading NW to the main P32 road, which is never far away. Shared taxis pass along this road every few minutes.

Apart from the flowers in spring, the main interest lies in the many ruined kasbahs along the route. A decline in the importance of agriculture, together with the inflow of money from overseas workers, has led to valley houses being abandoned for newer houses next to the main road. This, together with the disappearance of the extended family, has resulted in these fabulous buildings being left to rot. It is an eerie experience to wander around these places that seem largely intact, until one encounters a collapsed wall or pile of rubble.

Of particular note is the kasbah of El Gomte, near Imadnaghene. Unlike the other kasbahs passed en route this one is in a good state of preservation. It was built by the government during the last century and consists of two large kasbah buildings either side of a courtyard, surrounded by a large, intact, fortified wall. The high standard of construction and decoration (such as the green-tiled gateways) mark this as a special building.

## Escape Routes

In the event of accident or illness there are hospitals in Boumalne and Kelâa des Mgouna. They can be reached within a day from most parts of the trek. In addition there are medical facilities at the small mining town of Tiouit.

## From the Eastern Section of the Circuit: Igli - Tiouit

From Igli follow the route as described on day 6 to the gap between Tassigdelt Tamajgalt and its western neighbour (1hr.40mins.). Continue as for this route as far as the right-angled bend at the wadi (1hr.50mins.). Turn R up the little tributary. Follow this in amongst rock outcrops, generally ENE, for 400 metres before the path quits the bed for the R bank. Go over a small rise to regain the wadi bed. These are the northern slopes of Tassigdelt Tamajgalt and are very barren.

30 mins after leaving the main trail, the tributary ends in a cwm, the track takes the gap in the continuation line (NE). Drop steeply down into a deep valley, walk straight across this and up the opposite bank. You are now in a region of quartzite, and the landscape changes noticeably; steep, shattered crags reminiscent of the Toubkal region. Go up over the rocky crest to overlook a deep branch of the same valley you have just left (1hr., 2hrs.50mins. in total).

Walk along the L flank of this valley on a horizontal traverse. The rocky peak on the R is Azlou (2,215m). Fields come into view on the opposite bank after 3hrs. and seem out of place in this wild landscape. Descend, and at the furthest field take the RH valley branch (3hrs.05mins.). The LH branch leads to the Tizi-n'Irgounene. By 2 large fig trees and a rock pool (3hrs.20mins.) the path starts to climb the R bank. After 3hrs.50mins. you emerge onto a broad saddle. 1km or so ahead is a very prominent white blockhouse and mast on top of a steep rocky peak (Tadmamt, 2,491m). On the R in the distance the Tizi-n'Tazazert road is visible.

Trend generally NE on a level track to another saddle (4hrs.05mins.). The road is now clearly visible. Iknion comes into view in the distance, just to the L of Tadmamt. A magnificent view unfolds with the High Atlas to the N, and the long crest of Jebel Fengour (2,552m) and Amalou n'Mansour (2,712m) to the E above Iknion. A further 5-10mins. brings mine workings into view - a very incongruous sight. Continue down the dirt road until Tiouit is revealed nestling in its bowl.

This gold and copper mining town of 400 workers has an infirmary, telephone and shop. If more comprehensive medical facilities are required continue to Boumalne, 2hrs. by Land Rover down a dirt road. The staff at the mine are very helpful, in the past I have been given coffee and almonds in the manager's house whilst a driver was found to take me down to Boumalne.

## From the Central Part of the Circuit: Irhissi via Tizi-n'Tmirhcht to Dades Valley

This is a long day's walk, but by walking briskly it can be accomplished in 6-8hrs.. Until the Dades river plain is reached the route heads roughly N the whole way.

From the ruins at Irhissi head N up the valley for 25mins. until a zig-zag track is reached. Follow this, tortuously, on a good track to gain the summit col of the Tizi-n'Tmirhcht. Ahead the route is obvious - it takes the deep valley to where it intersects with a bigger E-W valley, then heads straight up the other side to a further prominent col (the Tizi-n'Irhioui). This is not as far as it looks, and the ground between the two cols can be covered in an hour.

From the Tizi-n'Irhioui descend into the valley to where the hills peter out and it emerges onto the stony plain. The best plan now is just to head out in a NE direction to gain the river as quickly as possible, cross this and on up to the main P32 road. **N.B.** At this point Kelâa des Mgouna is closer than Boumalne.

117

# PART SIX
## Other Areas

The following areas deserve a brief outline as places of potential interest to the trekker. They are mainly well off the beaten track, although parts of the eastern High Atlas are popular with the French.

### Jebel Siroua (3,305m)
An isolated peak on the edge of the Souss, it is an extinct volcano visible from many of the High Atlas peaks in the Toubkal region. It is covered on the 1:100,000 Taliwine map.

Reaching Siroua is difficult, and for this reason it is rarely climbed. The best approach is to start from Taliwine and follow dirt roads to the Magous gorge, 5 or 6 miles beyond Askaoun. From here, you can ascend the summit and return to the vehicle in one long day.

### The Western High Atlas
A beautiful area, perhaps the least frequented by walkers of the main Atlas regions. The walking here tends to be less strenuous than in the Toubkal or Mgoun areas. The climate is noticeably wetter due to the proximity of the ocean and, consequently, the vegetation is lusher and greener. Spring is a rewarding time to visit. The area is easily reached from Agadir; the town of Argana just off the main Agadir-Marrakech road is a suitable steeping-off point.

Notable peaks include Ras Moulay Ali (3,349m), Jebel Aoulime (3,555m) and the Tichka plateau. The area is bisected by fertile valleys and there are several gorges which provide exciting descents. The peaks Jebel Igdet (3,616m), the highest point in the western High Atlas, is best approached from the summit of the Tizi-n'Test.

### The Eastern High Atlas
Without doubt the most popular base for exploring the area is Imilchil with its shops, restaurants and mules for hire.

Just north of Imilchil is the beautiful Plateau des Lacs, which provides fine walking. Of the peaks **Jebel Ayyashi (3,747m)** is the most sought-after and is a very popular ascent. It is best approached from the north, starting at the small village of Ayt Ouchen, situated on a dirt road between Midelt and Tizi-n'Zou, a few kilometres east of the latter.

The nearest large cities are Beni Mellal, Meknes and Fez; the region's proximity to the prosperous north of the country accounts for its popularity.

## The Todra and Dades Gorges

Both of these gorges lie on the southern flanks of the main High Atlas and are within easy reach of Boumalne. Whilst not strictly walking country, they are spectacular and well worth a visit.

## The Todra Gorge

This is situated just N of Tinerhir, some 80 kilometres E of Boumalne on the P32. A good road leads into the gorge proper as far as a natural spring where the river emerges. At this point bulging cliffs (250m) of solid limestone tower above the gravel base of the canyon. The rock-climbing potential here is immense - masses of jamming cracks up steep walls, and pocketed limestone faces. The winter climate, also, is enviable. There is a hotel, Hotel Yasmin, situated (literally) under the largest cliff in the gorge narrows. A very cheap dormitory room is available and good meals are served.

Above the roadhead a 4-wheel drive vehicle is needed. It is possible to drive in 4-5hrs. across awful roads, via Msemrir, to gain the upper section of the Dades gorges.

## The Dades Gorges

These are situated N of Boumalne. Less visited than the Todra gorge they can be viewed from a rough road which follows their length. There is much more water flowing in this river and it has several good swimming-holes. Where the road leaves the gorge bottom in the upper part of the gorges, there is an exciting rappel/swim descent which leads on from this point. As long as it is warm enough this should present no difficulties.

# APPENDIX

## The Grand Traverse of the Atlas

This route devised by Michel Peyron (see bibliography) stretches from the western High Atlas at Imi-n'Tanout, to Taza in the NE. The complete traverse would be a major undertaking of 5 to 6 weeks duration, providing an extremely varied and enjoyable traverse. It can of course be done over several visits. It is of a moderate level of difficulty, forsaking the high ridges for passes in most instances. Numerous variations are described in Peyron's book.

## Ski-touring Possibilities

In wintertime the whole of the Atlas provides almost unlimited scope for ski-touring and is already popular with the Swiss and French, who come here seeking a change from the crowded European scene. January can often have bad weather, with February more settled. Good snow conditions can remain through to March and even April, although spring comes early to the Atlas warm sun can produce unpleasantly mushy conditions.

By and large the High Atlas are not very good for pure Langlauf, there is too little flat ground. The area lends itself to ski-mountaineering and cannot really be recommended to the beginner. In fact popular areas, such as the Neltner refuge, are too steep even for Telemark skis - skins, mountaineering bindings and *Harscheissen* are essential.

There is a French guidebook to the area (*Ski Randonnées dans le Haut Atlas Marocain*) obtainable in Oukaimeden which, with its ski tows and large plain, makes a good base for commencing any tour.

In the central High Atlas the Mgoun area has some fantastic ridge possibilities, including that of Mgoun itself. The less craggy nature lends itself more to ski-touring, though once again it is probably better for ski-mountaineering than cross-country.

The eastern Middle Atlas between Skoura and Taza are reputed to have a super ski-touring area at Bou Iblan. Snow conditions here are often much better than those encountered further west. There is a very attractive old refuge at Taffert, (permanently wardened), which acts as a good base for tours.

120

## Useful Addresses

### In Britain:
Moroccan National Tourist Office, 174 Regent Street, London W1.

### In Morocco:
O.N.M.T. Tourist Office, Place Abd el-Moumen ben Ali (intersection Ave. Mohammed V & Blvd. Mohammed Zerktouni), Guêliz, Marrakech.

Syndicat d'Initiative, 176 Ave. Mohammed V, Guêliz, Marrakech.

*Car Hire: Avis,* 137 Ave. Mohammed V, Guêliz, and at airport.

*Hertz,* Palais El Badia, and at airport.

*Royal Air Maroc:* for re-confirmation - Hotel Asni, Marrakech.

For ticket purchases etc. - 197 Ave. Mohammed V, Guêliz, Marrakech.

## Bibliography

Brown, Hamish. *The Great Walking Adventure* (Constable):
A personal account of the Atlas by one of its most frequent visitors.

Brown, Hamish. *The Alpine Journal 1987 Vol.92 No.336:*
A description of a long ridge traverse in winter.

Clark, B. *Berber Village* (London 1959):
A detailed study of the way of life in a High Atlas community.

Landau, Rom. *The Kasbahs of Southern Morocco* (Faber & Faber 1969): A good account of the local architecture, otherwise of little interest.

Peyron, M. *La Grande Traversée de l'Atlas Marocain (G.T.A.M.):*
Originally written in French, this is now available in an English translation. It describes the classic long traverse of the Toubkal range and beyond.

Maxwell, Gavin. *Lords of the Atlas* (Longmans, London 1966):
A classic account of the rise and fall of the Glaoui tribe, it gives a good insight into life in the region during the period preceding the French protectorate. Highly recommended.

Peterson, R.T., Mountfort, G. & Hollom, P.A.D. *A Field Guide to the Birds of Britain and Europe* (Collins 1974).

Hollom, P.A.D., Porter, R., Christensen, S. & Willis, I. *The Birds of the Middle East and North Africa* (Poyser 1988). Designed to be used in conjunction with the previous book, together they describe every species of bird to be found in the region.

**Glossary**

Below is a list of words, both Arabic and Berber, one is most likely to encounter in speech or as map features.

| | |
|---|---|
| Adrar (Ber.) | mountain |
| Aguelman (Ber.) | lake |
| Ain (Ar.) *pl.* Aioun | spring |
| Ait (Ber.) | tribe (sons of) |
| Assif (Ber.) | river |
| Azib (Ber.) | summer hut |
| Bab (Ar.) | gateway, mouth |
| Hammam (Ar) | steam-bath |
| Imi (Ber.) | gateway, mouth |
| Irhil (Ar.) | mountain massif |
| Kasbah (Ar.) | fortified house, or village |
| Ksar (Ar.) *pl.* Ksour | castle, walled stronghold |
| Marabout (Ar.) | shrine |
| Oued (Ar.) | river or valley |
| Sidi, seti (Ar.) | saint |
| Tizi (Ber.) | col, pass |

*Arabic Numbers:*

| | | | |
|---|---|---|---|
| 1 Waha | 2 Juje | 3 Tlettãa | 4 Rabãa |
| 5 Qhamsa | 6 Seta | 7 Sebãa | 8 Temenya |
| 9 Tis-aa | 10 Ashara | 11 Qadãash | 12 Tnãash |
| 13 Tlettãash | 14 Rabãatsh | 15 Qhamstãash | 16 Stãash |
| 17 Sebatãash | 18 Tementãash | 19 Tisatãash | 20 Ashareen |
| 30 Tletteen | 40 Rabaa-een | 50 Qhamseen | 60 Seteen |
| 70 'Seba-een | 80 Temenyeen | 90 T'saeen | 100 Meeya |
| 200 Meetayn | | | |
| 300 Tletmeeya | | | |
| 400 Rabaameeya | | | |
| 1000 Elf | | | |